Gladys

O9-CFT-897

486 N. Liberty St.

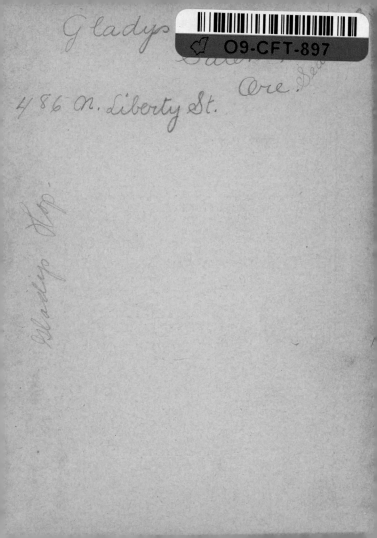

LOWELL'S

THE VISION OF SIR LAUNFAL

AND OTHER POEMS

Macmillan's Pocket American and English Classics

A Series of English Texts, edited for use in Elementary and Secondary Schools, with Critical Introductions, Notes, etc.

16mo   Cloth   25 cents each

Addison's Sir Roger de Coverley.

Andersen's Fairy Tales.

Arabian Nights' Entertainments.

Arnold's Sohrab and Rustum.

Bacon's Essays.

Bible (Memorable Passages from).

Blackmore's Lorna Doone.

Browning's Shorter Poems.

Browning, Mrs., Poems (Selected).

Bryant's Thanatopsis, etc.

Bunyan's The Pilgrim's Progress.

Burke's Speech on Conciliation.

Burns' Poems (Selections from).

Byron's Childe Harold's Pilgrimage.

Byron's Shorter Poems.

Carlyle's Essay on Burns.

Carlyle's Heroes and Hero Worship.

Carroll's Alice's Adventures in Wonderland (Illustrated).

Chaucer's Prologue and Knight's Tale.

Church's The Story of the Iliad.

Church's The Story of the Odyssey.

Coleridge's The Ancient Mariner.

Cooper's The Deerslayer.

Cooper's The Last of the Mohicans.

Defoe's Robinson Crusoe.

De Quincey's Confessions of an English Opium-Eater.

De Quincey's Joan of Arc, and The English Mail-Coach.

Dickens' A Christmas Carol, and The Cricket on the Hearth.

Dickens' A Tale of Two Cities.

Dryden's Palamon and Arcite.

Early American Orations, 1760-1824.

Edwards' (Jonathan) Sermons.

Eliot's Silas Marner.

Emerson's Essays.

Emerson's Representative Men.

Epoch-making Papers in U. S. History.

Franklin's Autobiography.

Gaskell's Cranford.

Goldsmith's The Deserted Village.

Goldsmith's The Vicar of Wakefield.

Grimm's Fairy Tales.

Hawthorne's Grandfather's Chair.

Hawthorne's Tanglewood Tales.

Hawthorne's The House of the Seven Gables.

Hawthorne's Twice-told Tales (Selections from).

Hawthorne's Wonder-Book.

Holmes' Poems.

Homer's Iliad (Translated).

Homer's Odyssey (Translated).

Irving's Life of Goldsmith.

Irving's The Alhambra.

Irving's Sketch Book.

Keary's Heroes of Asgard.

Macmillan's Pocket American and English Classics

A Series of English Texts, edited for use in Elementary and Secondary Schools, with Critical Introductions, Notes, etc.

16mo   Cloth   25 cents each

Kingsley's The Heroes.
Lamb's The Essays of Elia.
Longfellow's Evangeline.
Longfellow's Hiawatha.
Longfellow's Miles Standish.
Longfellow's Tales of a Wayside Inn.
Lowell's The Vision of Sir Launfal.
Macaulay's Essay on Addison.
Macaulay's Essay on Hastings.
Macaulay's Essay on Lord Clive.
Macaulay's Essay on Milton.
Macaulay's Lays of Ancient Rome.
Macaulay's Life of Samuel Johnson.
Milton's Comus and Other Poems.
Milton's Paradise Lost, Books I. and II.
Old English Ballads.
Out of the Northland.
Palgrave's Golden Treasury.
Plutarch's Lives (Cæsar, Brutus, and Mark Antony).
Poe's Poems.
Poe's Prose Tales (Selections from).
Pope's Homer's Iliad.
Pope's The Rape of the Lock.
Ruskin's Sesame and Lilies.
Scott's Ivanhoe.
Scott's Kenilworth.
Scott's Lady of the Lake.

Scott's Lay of the Last Minstrel.
Scott's Marmion.
Scott's Quentin Durward.
Scott's The Talisman.
Shakespeare's As You Like It.
Shakespeare's Hamlet.
Shakespeare's Henry V.
Shakespeare's Julius Cæsar.
Shakespeare's King Lear.
Shakespeare's Macbeth.
Shakespeare's Merchant of Venice.
Shakespeare's The Tempest.
Shakespeare's Twelfth Night.
Shelley and Keats: Poems.
Sheridan's The Rivals and The School for Scandal.
Southern Poets: Selections.
Spenser's Faerie Queene, Book I.
Stevenson's The Master of Ballantrae.
Stevenson's Treasure Island.
Swift's Gulliver's Travels.
Tennyson's Idylls of the King.
Tennyson's The Princess.
Tennyson's Shorter Poems.
Thackeray's Henry Esmond.
Washington's Farewell Address, and Webster's First Bunker Hill Oration.
Woolman's Journal.
Wordsworth's Shorter Poems.

·The· M Co·

JAMES RUSSELL LOWELL.

THE

VISION OF SIR LAUNFAL

AND OTHER POEMS

BY

JAMES RUSSELL LOWELL

EDITED WITH NOTES AND INTRODUCTION

BY

HERBERT BATES

TEACHER OF ENGLISH, MANUAL TRAINING HIGH SCHOOL
BROOKLYN, N.Y.

New York
THE MACMILLAN COMPANY
LONDON: MACMILLAN & CO., Ltd.
1908

PREFATORY NOTE

The object that I have set before myself in editing this poem is that which directs my teaching it in the classroom. This object is compounded of several elements. First of all, the pupil should understand the poem, should get from it the meaning that the poet put into it. He should, secondly, draw from it something of the imaginative elevation that inspired the poet to its composition. Thirdly, mingled with these, he should get some perception of the character, the personal magnetism, of the author, — should feel him speaking through his poem.

Incidental to this there should be explanation of words, comment on verse-forms, — all that minor detail that it is folly to despise, and still greater folly to overestimate. Over all should stand the main pur-

pose, — to explain and enforce the dual message of
the poet: —

> " Not only around our infancy,
>   Doth heaven with all its splendors lie,"

and, —

> " Not that which we give, but what we share,
>   For the gift without the giver is bare."

To make the pupils understand this and feel it, feel it
in the spirit of the man that gave it utterance, this
should be the ideal alike of editor and teacher.

In teaching the poem in class, it will be found
helpful to devote one lesson to the poem as a whole
before taking it up in detail. This will make clearer
its main purpose and emphasize its message. But
most important and hardest, one must avoid a shrink-
ing tendency to keep the poem's highest meaning and
inspiration for the tabernacle of one's own heart,
leaving the class to seek this for themselves, and
putting before them only the dry husks of verbal
elucidation. It is the height of egotism to regard the
higher enjoyment of poetry as the perquisite of the

æsthetically elect.   In each soul there lurks some seed of poetry, a seed that quickens responsive to the warm influence of the true poet.   It is for us to bring these seeds to this sunlight, — to develop, with unabashed idealism, a human tendency that may defeat the material greed that endangers modern life, — to arouse the divine discontent that looks beyond the partial, which is, to the perfect, which may be.

H. B.

CONTENTS

	PAGE
PREFATORY NOTE	V

INTRODUCTION.

The Poet and his Surroundings	ix
The Vision of Sir Launfal	xxxiv
Bibliography	xxxix
Subjects for Composition	xli

POEMS.

The Vision of Sir Launfal	1
An Indian Summer Reverie	18
Rhœcus	33
The Bobolink	40
To the Dandelion	45
An Incident in a Railroad Car	48
Lines, suggested by the Graves of Two English Soldiers	53
The Shepherd of King Admetus	56
The Beggar	59

		PAGE
Beaver Brook	.	62
My Love	.	65
The Birch Tree	.	68
The Sirens	.	70
√ The Courtin'	.	75
The Changeling	.	78
NOTES	.	81
INDEX	.	123

INTRODUCTION

THE POET AND HIS SURROUNDINGS

Of American poets Lowell is one of the most American. Wiser than the eccentric Whitman, wiser than our writers of *Columbiads* and epics of the red Indian, Lowell saw that the real American is not a new being, cut off from the literary tradition of the past. The American is the Englishman in a new world. He has brought with him the language, the traditions, the mental characteristics, the instincts of his ancestors; and he has modified these in accordance with his new environment. He has carried the old life into a new land, and the result, though with something of a "sea-change," is not wholly "new or strange."

Lowell stands, aggressively, perhaps, for the American of English descent, for the American whose "forbears" left England to carry on in a new country the spirit of the old. Few of our poets have studied with greater diligence the models of the past. Few have turned their eyes with such painstaking fidelity to the life about us. For Lowell's world is not conventional.

He does not give us laboriously imagined pictures of England or of Scotland. We have instead, "the hang-bird nests on the elm tree bough," "the icehouse-girdled pond," "half ventu'in' liverworts in furry coats," or "the catbird in the laylock bush." "Not ours," he tells us, "is the Old World's good" or the Old World's ill. We live our own life, with its own native ideals, in a land whose least details appeal to associated emotions.

In the *Pictures from Appledore,* an *Indian Summer Reverie, Under the Willows,* the poem on schooldays in the introduction to the first series of the *Biglow Papers,* — in all these, and in many others, one finds Lowell's love for the sights that he saw as a child, — that delighted wonder, that capability for rapture in little things, which makes the poet. It is not the things of which he reads that inspire him, — it is the things that he sees. And to us, who see and delight in the same sights that delighted him, his verse should appeal with deep-felt directness.

Conspicuous in Lowell's writings is his sense of humor. Not that, like many writers, he is inclined to separate the two rôles, poet and humorist; whatever he may have said of his "dual nature," Lowell saw beauty and imagined ideals with the same eyes with which he noted oddities of character or detected the absurdities of pretence. His humor is American, keen, kindly, wholesome,— earth-born, yet heaven-seeking; never hesitating to proclaim truths however unheard of, to denounce falsehoods however established. In such a spirit lies safety. No sham can flourish in its presence, no wind-bag of grandiloquence resist its thrust. It is the humor, saving, through-seeing, nation-guiding, that gleams from the shrewd face of Franklin, or that smiles at us half sadly from the eyes of Lincoln.

No man possessing keenly this sense can fall deeply into sentimentality. The tearful sentimentalist takes himself with deadly seriousness. To Lowell the amiable insipidities of Willis and Percival were impossible. One half of his nature was on the watch to catch the other half in a pretence. In his letters jest and sober speculation mingle, but do not conflict. Honest humor and wholesome wit — not the cheap sneering that some think witty — can never be irreconcilable with any serious thought worth the thinking. Lowell is the same man in his letters as in his poems. There is no pose to be put off, no mask to be laid aside. He is, in all he writes, outspokenly himself.

Another element to be noted throughout his work is its youth. Shelley has been spoken of as the "eternal child." Perhaps all poets — all of real vitality — must have this eternity of childhood, this protracting of the wonder at the world and delight in it that all feel in childhood, but that for most of us too soon passes, to "fade into the light of common day." He realized vividly, himself, his youth of spirit. He never, he says in one of his letters, could get to consider himself as anything more than a boy. His temperament was so youthful that whenever people solemnly consulted him, as if his opinion were worth anything, he could hardly help laughing. And he would think to himself, with a suppressed laugh, that the grave inquirer would be "as mad as a hornet" if he knew that he was consulting in reality a boy of twelve, masked by a "bearded visor." And in a letter, written in his old age, he jots down an imaginary anecdote about himself, telling how, passing a "Hospital for Incurable Children," he turned to his companion and said quietly, "There's where they'll send me one of these days."

It is this frank retention of the best of childhood, — its power of delight, its capacity of wonder, its sensitive nearness to the God of nature, that speaks out in the Prelude to the *Sir Launfal*. The prophecies of the great winds, the benedicite of the druid wood, spoke, in him, to ears that hardly needed the reveille of their spiritual summons. For the poet is he who hears, with ears quickened to the heavenly accents, the mighty voice of unsuspected Sinais, and is its interpreter to men.

There is also to be noted in his work — not unrelated to his undying sense of youthful wonder — a certain mysticism, — a dominating sense of the spiritual world, a sense possibly inherited from Puritan ancestors, which he himself, however, used to trace remotely to his mother's Celtic forefathers in the days of the Scotch Sir Patrick Spens. "One half of me," he wrote to a friend, "was clear mystic and enthusiast." If he had lived in solitude, like the hermits of the Thebais, he had no doubt that he, with them, might have had authentic interviews with the evil one, — and it might indeed have taken but little to make a St. Francis of him. He was never — when alone — a single night unvisited by visions, and once was convinced that he had a personal revelation from God himself. Not a meteor could fall, nor lightning flash, that he did not in some way connect it with his own spiritual life and destiny.

He speaks, at another time, of a "revelation." He was talking, among friends, of the presence of spirits when suddenly, as he was speaking, the whole system of things stood clear before him "like a vague Destiny looming from the abyss." He felt the spirit of God present in and around him, filling the very room with Pentecostal power, making the air itself vibrate with its mighty presence. And even his words, as he spoke to those about him, seemed filled with an influence greater than himself.

It is these qualities that characterize his work. And
all these elements were brought into activity under the
influence of the new movement in English literature, —
the movement of the new or Romantic poets. Wordsworth, Coleridge, Keats, Shelley, Byron, Scott, — all
these had broken into song, a new irregular song,
shaking off the fetters of the formal couplet, shaking
off, too, the artificiality that went with the traditions
of Pope and Johnson, and the echo of this new song,
reaching America, roused like music in the hearts of
our singers here. In our Cambridge group we find
the American response to the inspiration of the Lake
circle of English singers of half a century before, and
of this new-world group Lowell best caught the finer,
more ethereal tone. He approaches nearest to the
divine dreams of Coleridge.

His poetry is, of course, not without its defects. His
verse is not always musical, though he himself had great
confidence in his ear. He might be a bad poet, he said,
but he declared that he was a good versifier, and wrote
with far more ease in verse than in prose. He had
studied the subject of versification from beginning to
end, and if his poems contained any rough verses, these
were intentional. He laid the whole blame on the
readers. Yet if the readers went astray, Lowell was
really to blame. He left too much to their ears.
Knowing how he wanted his lines to sound, he failed

to see that the clew to their rhythmic structure was not obvious. It is not enough that a verse can be read correctly; it must be so constructed that the reader will find it almost impossible to go wrong.

But Lowell's great merit, the excellence that lifts his poetry to the level of really great song, is his compelling perception of eternal truth. His writings abound in quick "flashes," "jewels five words long," thoughts immortally incarnate in ringing epigram. In his prose, in his verse, the same swift power thrills us, — the indefinable unexpectedness of genius.

Such, in quick survey, was the character and genius of Lowell. Look now, rapidly, at the main facts of his life, — at those, especially, that bear on his poetic activity.

Lowell was born in 1819, twelve years after Longfellow. His boyhood is significant. The Cambridge of Lowell's youth was not the Cambridge of to-day. Now one sees busy streets lined with crowded houses; trolley cars rattle by; one must go miles to find the unspoiled country. But the Cambridge of 1830 was the quiet rustic village. In his *Thirty Years Ago*, Lowell describes it as seen from Symond's Hill, on the New Road, the road that followed the river from Watertown. The picture is different to-day, for the hand of man has made many changes, but the general outlines are the same. In the foreground then lay the

town buried in elms, lindens, and horse-chestnuts, —
old trees that had stood there when George the Third
was king, and that could not, like the Tories that
planted them, take disgusted leave of the new republic.
Above these stood out the college belfry, the square
brown tower of Christ Church, the slim spire of
the meeting-house — the invariable landmark of every
New England village. Off to the right could be seen
the Charles, winding in broad curves through its em-
purpled salt-marshes, with their shifting play of light
and shade. Beyond these rose, as now, the gently
rounded hills of Brookline.

At the end of the New Road towered the six huge
willows, made memorable by Lowell in his poem, *Under
the Willows :* —

> " Six, a willow Pleiades,
> The seventh fallen, that lean along the brink
> Where the steep upland dips into the marsh."

It is to these trees, too, that he refers in the *Indian
Summer Reverie* (see lines 253–259). In this *Reverie,*
in *Under the Willows,* and in the poem on the school-
house, the poem ascribed to Hosea Biglow and inserted
in the introduction to the first series of the *Biglow
Papers,* we find many details of the country scenes
that Lowell knew as a boy. In the latter we find this
glimpse : —

" Ah, dear old times ! how brightly ye return !
How, rubbed afresh, your phosphor traces burn !
The ramble schoolward through dewsparkling meads,
The willow-wands turned Cinderella steeds ;
The impromptu pinbent hook, the deep remorse
O'er the chance-captured minnow's inchlong corse ;
The pockets, plethoric with marbles round,
That still a space for ball and peg-top found,
Nor satiate yet, could manage to confine
Horse-chestnuts, flagroot, and the kite's wound twine,
And, like the prophet's carpet could take in,
Enlarging still, the popgun's magazine ;
The dinner carried in the small tin pail,
Shared with the dog, whose most beseeching tail
And dripping tongue and eager eyes belied
The assumed indifference of canine pride.
. . . .

Dropped at the corner of the embowered lane,
Whistling I wade the knee-deep leaves again,
While eager Argus, who has missed all day
The sharer of his condescending play,
Comes leaping forward with a bark elate
And boisterous tail to greet me at the gate."

One can imagine endless details of the life of the
country boy. In winter there was coasting and skat-
ing ; in summer he could pitch hay, pick berries, wade
in the brooks, wander in the woods or along the river.
Any country boy can supply the rest. But there was
one element in his country life that not every country
boy, not every New England boy, can supply. For

the boy Lowell, with his sensitiveness to beauty, his love of nature, must have found in woods, waters, hills, and skies, a charm that to the thousands of others that saw them was unfelt, or was felt in less degree. The poet does not spend his boyhood in indifference to the beauty about him and then suddenly, with the assumption of his poetic rôle, take up appreciation of nature as a profession. His delight, on the contrary, has been with him from the first. The blue of the sky, the song of a bird, the rapid flight of a cloud, the green blaze of the new grass, the flame of the November maple, stir him with an intensity of rapture unfelt by his fellows, and it is this intensity of feeling that drives him, sooner or later, to poetic expression. Lowell observed nature, not because he had decided to be a poet, but because the intensity of his perceptions, his ecstacy in the beauty about him, made him, and would have made him, even had he willed otherwise, the poet that he was. For it was in his boyhood that Lowell learned his poetry, — not the art of expression in rhyme and metre; that he had to acquire little by little, — but the impressions, the pictures, the dreams that live in his lines. These he absorbed, unconsciously, in the fields, woods, and hillsides of that quiet New England town, with its river ebbing indolently seaward, or bringing back, with the flood, waifs of seaweed and scents of the sea.

But his youth was surrounded by something besides the picturesque present of wood and river. About it lay the romance of bygone days. Elmwood was of colonial date, a stately mansion, with wide lands about it and majestic elms arching over it. Such a house is full of the best of the past, — not its decay, but its wealth of association.

It was, so Lowell says, about twice as old as himself. Around it lay some ten acres of open land, and some fine old trees, pine and elm. It was square — four rooms to a floor, and, like all of the old Tory mansions, solidly built, with massive oaken beams, the spaces filled in with brick. For all its trees, it was a sunny house, the sun getting — in the course of the day — a glimpse at every side of it. Within, if you followed up the straight path between the lilacs, and entered, was a quaint staircase with twisted banisters. The rooms were moderately large, "sixteen feet square, and, on the ground floor, nine feet high." While not palatial, it had, like all houses of its type, a stately self-content, an "air of amplitude as from some inward sense of dignity."

The boy Lowell had slept in a garret room, and about the time that the poet wrote the *Vision*, he had returned to this. Here he dreamt dreams and saw visions as he lay alone in the dark, for his mother would not allow him to have a light. She wanted him to learn not to fear the darkness, and he learned his lesson, though at first in terror, hiding his head under the pillows to shut out the shapeless monsters that his fancy saw thronging round him. But the room was not always dark, — the sun shone upon its windows, from which in winter the boy could look out across the wide marshes of the Charles, brown and barren or buried under white levels of glittering snow.

As spring came on, however, the leaves shut out, bit by bit, all this spacious landscape, till, in May, the poet wrote sequestered from all distraction in a "cool and restful privacy of leaves."

Lowell's first school-days were spent in the " dame-school," described in the introduction to the *Biglow Papers.*

> " Propt on the marsh, a dwelling now, I see
> The humble school-house of my A. B. C.,
> Where well-drilled urchins, each behind his tire,
> Waited in ranks the wished command to fire,
> Then all together, when the signal came,
> Discharged their *a-b abs* against the dame. . . .
> She mid the volleyed learning firm and calm,
> Patted the furloughed ferule on her palm,
> And, to our wonder, could divine at once
> Who flashed the pan, and who was downright dunce."

The next step was his being sent, as a day-scholar, to the boarding-school of Mr. William Wells, an Englishman, who, so far as conditions allowed, carried on his school under the disciplinary traditions of the English schools. He was severe but, fortunately for his pupils, thorough, and Lowell's Latin shows the result of his training. In the collection of Lowell's letters we find a few written during his attendance there. They are very boyish, without the remotest evidence of genius, containing, for example, the information that the writer had "the ague together with a gumbile," that his mother has given him three volumes of "tales of a grandfather," and that the master had not taken his rattan out since the vacation.

This school was near Lowell's home. So was Harvard College, — at least only a mile away, so that when he attended there he was able to spend the night at home. He entered college at the age of fifteen, — not so remarkably early an age for entrance as it is now. Pupils entered younger then. The college buildings had always been a familiar sight to the boy —

> "There in red brick, which softening time defies,
> Stand square and stiff, the Muses' factories."

His entrance did not compel that breaking of former ties that we find in the lives of others. It was but a new element entering into the old life.

One can trace the influence of his college life upon

his work. Probably the teaching of Professor Channing had no little effect upon his English, as well as upon that of other well-known writers who were at Harvard in those days. Professor Channing, Dr. Hale tells us, met his pupils "face to face and hand to hand," talking over their work with them, with shrewd admonition and kindly irony. Note, too, that it was in Lowell's sophomore year that the young Longfellow entered upon his professorship, with poetic prestige already won, brought into stimulating companionship with students hardly younger than himself.

The influence of contemporary literature was strongly felt, — not the literature prescribed in the curriculum, but literature to which the young men turned of their own eagerness, new live literature, marking the inception and inspiring the development of a new era. Novels innumerable were read and discussed. The defiant recklessness of Byron had still its malign charm. The poems of Keats, Shelley, Coleridge, were not only read, but were memorized, absorbed, to be given out again in varied incarnation. Carlyle's works were appreciated here long before they found appreciation in England, and Tennyson's first thin volume, borrowed from Emerson, was " passed reverently from hand to hand," while some poems were passed from student to student in manuscript, as a new ode by Horace might have circulated among the young enthusiasts of Rome.

Literature, in short, was the fashion, — as athletics seems to be the fashion now, — and this indulgence had the added charm of being forbidden. Not that the reading itself was forbidden; the zest lay in the manner of enjoyment. Secret societies were at that time proscribed in Harvard. Nevertheless we learn, thanks to Dr. Hale's confessions, that the Alpha Delta Phi led a delightful and unsuspected existence under the very eyes of the authorities. In its room, to which each member had a pass-key, the small circle of the elect read, studied, held literary meetings, and developed that united enthusiasm, that certainty of sympathy, that goes so far toward the making of literature.

This society, with the editorship of the college magazine, *Harvardiana*, made up a conspicuous part of Lowell's college life. To this, of course, must be added the regular scholastic work, the diversion of evening parties, and, now and then, a stroll in the country or an excursion to the seashore.

Lowell's graduation was not brilliant. Not that he was incapable of application; his later work is evidence enough of his diligence. No poet had less of the dreamy inefficiency of a Coleridge. Nor was his literary genius unrecognized. The year Lowell graduated, Dr. Hale tells us, his friends were as sure as all are now that in him was first-rate poetical genius, and that he was to be one of the leaders of literature. The trouble was, in part, that such work as most attracted him was not in those days recognized in the college curriculum. English literature was not formally studied, and the reading that best prepared him for his life-work least prepared him for the artificial exigencies of examination. But this, with his quick intelligence, was not enough materially to impair his standing. The great trouble lay in recklessness with regard to chapel attendance. Chapel in those days was compulsory, and Lowell "cut" six days out of seven. His regularity of reform on the one day — Monday of each week — naturally counted nothing in his favor, and he was summarily "rusticated," that is, sent to live in the rural retirement of Concord. Here, under the staid care of the Rev. Barzillai Frost, he memorized pages of *Locke on the Human Understanding,* and thought of the approaching delights of the August class-day, — delights not for him. What made exile especially bitter was that he was class-poet. His poem had to be omitted from the exercises, and he had to console himself with the warm sympathy that students extend to those afflicted by authority.

After graduation we find Lowell hesitating as to

his future. He had promised his father that he would "give up poetry and go to work." So he plunged into the study of the law. He completed his studies, — for he was diligent, — and even went so far as to rent an office and hang out a sign. Rumor reports that he had a client. It appears from his letters that he wrote some verses that were to win for his broken-hearted Carolinian client the affections of some cold Southern beauty, but this "case" was not strictly professional. Whatever his success, his inclinations soon led him to forsake the law for literature.

In the very small Boston of 1838, where everybody knew everybody, it was not hard for a writer of merit to gain recognition. To gain a livelihood was another matter. Except for the *North American Review* — which unfortunately was not yet in accord with the new spirit — few magazines then paid for articles. Young writers must make magazines for themselves, apologetic magazinelettes that tried to live without advertising matter, and that died promptly of sheer starvation. *The Miscellany* was one of these. *The Pioneer* followed it to a speedy death. Yet both contained names that would make the fortune of a modern publisher, — Lowell, Hawthorne, Poe, — of writers then unrecognized, but sure of future recognition.

More important than the actual publication of work
was the intimate association of the young authors.
What the secret society had done in their college
days was carried on by another organization of young
men and young women — boys and girls, one might
almost say — united in such wholesome companionship as Miss Alcott loves to depict in her stories.
The girls called this society the "Band"; the boys
preferred to call it the "Club." It was not so much
a society as a friendship. The home of each was the
home of all. "Among the ten there was the simplest
and most absolute personal friendship." Their meetings were informal, and their entertainment ranged
from ecstacy over the sonnets of Shakespeare to tune-
less and obstreperous choruses of nonsense-songs. It
was a group of young people, full of alert life, filled,
too, with ardent enthusiasm and high aspiration.

A group so spiritual could not fail to be moved by
the anti-slavery agitation. Lowell at first had cared
little about this, but we find his interest increasing,
till, partly through the influence of Maria White, he
became an active worker, closely associated with Gar-
rison, Whittier, and other outspoken abolitionists.

It is about this time that Maria White becomes
prominent in his life. At their very first meeting she
seems to have impressed him deeply. All who knew
her seem to have felt the charm of her personality.

Her picture shows a delicate girlish face, spiritual, nobly beautiful. Lowell tells of a talk with a farmer, a brown-faced giant, whose simple nature was profoundly moved by her spiritual beauty. He had never seen such a face. There was, he felt, as he told Lowell, "something supernatural" about it, something "heavenly and angelic."

It was in the time of his engagement and in the earlier years of his marriage that we find Lowell's poetic powers most active. His first volume of poems was published in 1841. It was called *A Year's Life*. It included little of his best work. In fact, his genius had still to "find itself," his writings were still imitative and experimental. Yet in this volume one finds such strong feeling as that of *Threnodia*, such delicacy as is shown in the *Sirens*, for all its reminiscence of Tennyson, and the sparkling delight of the *Fountain*. A second series followed a few years later, with decided gain in poetic individuality.

There was a practical need for such gain. It was no longer a matter of small concern what work the young poet should take up. His father's affairs had become such that he must make money — or go hungry. And this practical necessity seems to have operated as a not unkindly stimulus. He plunged into his work with a new energy, an energy that resulted in the production of some of his best work.

The period of the writing of *Sir Launfal* was for
Lowell, what the year of the production of the *Ancient
Mariner* was for Coleridge. In it he awakened to
fuller realization of his own powers. His marriage,
in 1844, had brought into his life a new sympathy,
a new confidence and ambition. It had brought,
too, a livelier interest in public affairs, — an influence
that was to lead to the composition of the *Biglow
Papers.* We find him, at once, in several rôles, the
dreamer and preacher of the *Sir Launfal,* the humorist
of the *Fable for Critics,* and the patriot and reformer
of the *Biglow Papers.*

At the *Sir Launfal* we shall look later. Let us
glance for a moment at his other works. The *Fable
for Critics* was satire aimed at a real evil. American
literature had been stationary, resting complacently
on a mistaken sense of achievement. Read Gris-
wold's *American Poets* and you will get some idea of
the nobodies that were put on a level with the great
masters of literature. The worst of it was that it was
held to be patriotic to support their pretensions. Our
literary circles were mere mutual admiration societies.

With this spirit Lowell had no sympathy. In his
Fable, after an introduction, rollicking in puns, con-
ceits, and fantastic rhymes, he takes up one writer
after another and points out his merits and demerits,
— nor does he spare himself.

"There is Lowell, who's striving Parnassus to climb
  With a whole bale of *isms* tied together with rhyme. . .
  His lyre has some chords that would ring pretty well,
  But he'd rather by half make a drum of the shell,
  And rattle away till he's old as Methusalem
  At the head of a march to the last New Jerusalem."

With regard to the comparison with English authors, we find : —

"But what's that ? a mass meeting ?   No, there come in lots
  The American Disraelis, Bulwers, and Scotts,
  And, in short, the American everything-elses,
  Each charging the others with envies and jealousies ; —
  By the way, 'tis a fact that displays what profusions
  Of all kinds of greatness bless free institutions,
  That while the Old World has produced barely eight
  Of such poets as all men agree to call great. . . .
  With you every year a whole crop is begotten,
  They're as much of a staple as corn is, or cotton. . . .
  I myself know ten Byrons, one Coleridge, three Shelleys,
  Two Raphaels, six Titians, (I think) one Apelles,
  Leonardos and Rubenses plenty as lichens,
  One (but that one is plenty) American Dickens,
  A whole flock of Lambs, any number of Tennysons, —
  In short, if a man has the luck to have any sons,
  He may feel pretty certain that one out of twain
  Will be some very great person over again."

Lowell believed, and this belief was one of the
foundation-beliefs of his character, that the best

patriotism did not forbid fault-finding, but rather demanded it.

> "There are truths you Americans need to be told,
>   And it never'll refute them to swagger and scold."

And again,

> " I honor the man who is willing to sink
>   Half his present repute for the freedom to think,
>   And, when he has thought, be his cause strong or weak,
>   Will risk t'other half for the freedom to speak,
>   Caring nought for what vengeance the mob has in store,
>   Let that mob be the upper ten thousand or lower."

The spirit that made the *Fable for Critics* was the spirit that made the *Biglow Papers*. In one, literary pretence is denounced; in the other, national evils find treatment no less frank. The Mexican war Lowell felt to be a great wrong. He believed, so he wrote in a letter to Thomas Hughes, "that this war with Mexico (though he owned that we had as just a ground for it as a strong nation ever has against a weak) was essentially a war of false pretences, and would result in widening the boundaries and so prolonging the life of slavery. Lowell believed that it was the "manifest destiny" of the English race to occupy the whole North American continent ... but he hated to see "a noble hope evaporated into a lying phrase to

sweeten the foul breath of demagogues." Against
such an abuse he felt convinced that all honest men
should protest.

The papers, written in the dialect that Lowell had
heard among the country people about his home, were
spirited denunciations of the war and of those politi-
cians who advocated it. Hosea Biglow, an untutored
country lad, is supposed to be the writer, and his
utterances are accompanied by very pedantic comment
by the imaginary Parson Wilbur, a genial but over-
learned minister of the gospel. The great achievement
of these poems lies in the fact that, like the poetry of
Burns, they brought song into touch with life as it is
and brought poetic speech nearer to homely idiom.
This might not have been the case had the poems
confined themselves to their political theme. They
had, however, bits of another sort, scraps of living
nature, like the story of the *Courtin'* (see p. 75), or
the beautiful description of the coming of spring in
the *Second Series.*

For the political papers, one stanza may give some
taste of their plain-spoken vigor : —

> " Ez fer war, I call it murder, —
>   There you hev it plain an' flat ;
> I don't want to go no furder
>   Than my Testyment fer that ;

God hez sed so plump an' fairly,
    It's ez long ez it is broad,
An' you've gut to git up airly
    Ef you want to take in God.

" 'Taint your eppyletts an' feathers
    Make the thing a grain more right ;
'Taint afollerin' your bell-wethers
    Will excuse ye in His sight ;
Ef you take a sword an' dror it,
    An' go stick a feller thru,
Guv'ment ain't to answer for it,
    God'll send the bill to you."

It is from these poems, one may say, from the *Fable for Critics,* and from the *Sir Launfal* and the *Commemoration Ode,* that Lowell won his widest note. It is these, perhaps, that represent, better than others, the variety and scope of his poetic genius.

With Lowell's later life, students of the *Sir Launfal* are not so much concerned. True, the Lowell that wrote the poem had in him the elements that made him what he was later, — poet, critic, editor, professor, orator, scholar, and statesman. But these qualities only slightly affect the character of the poem. Here we can but glance at his varied activities.

Besides being editor of the two little magazines already mentioned, Lowell edited, for a time, the *North American Review.* His literary work, beyond this, extended itself in the direction of critical articles on various literary subjects, reviews, essays, studies of many kinds. The lecture system was at that time developing, and Lowell, like Emerson, played a strong part in its development. Many of his lectures appear in his published essays.

The professorship of modern languages at Harvard, though in some respects a disadvantage to Lowell's poetic genius, seems, like the years of foreign travel that preceded it, to have enlarged the whole nature of the man. He returned with more cosmopolitan standards, not less patriotic, — as some obstreperous " patriots " proclaimed him, — but more judicious in his patriotism. His scholarship undoubtedly restricted his creative power. Yet it was in itself memorable, and Harvard lost, in his resignation, not merely a stimulating teacher and inspiring singer, but a scholar who combined, as few can, accuracy with enthusiasm.

Lowell's ministry abroad, first in Spain, then in England, marks the last period of his life — if we except the rather pathetic postscript of the closing years at Elmwood. He filled the rôle with distinction and discretion. It was a loss to this country and a deprivation to England when political changes here made his withdrawal necessary. He won the respect of both countries by his tact and statesmanship.

His poetic work, in later life, affords great variety.

Besides the poems included in this volume, there is the majestic *Commemoration Ode*, one of the largest, in dignity of spirit, of all patriotic poems. There are the sharply sketched *Pictures from Appledore*, the thoughtful *Cathedral, Under the Willows*, with its exquisite pictures of home scenery, and many more, so many that it takes one long to discover all their beauties. Their merit is not even, but the merit of the best is memorable.

In conclusion : try in your study of these poems to see Lowell as a man, as a young man, such a young man as he was when he set down on paper the words of the *Vision*, a man filled as few are with the sense of the wonder of the world about us, and filled, moreover, with a spiritual perception of the imminence of Heaven, the pervading presence of God. It was such a man wrote this poem, and it was because he was such a man, open to all high impulses, that the poem is what it is, — a beautiful and inspiring utterance of a noble tenderness.

THE VISION OF SIR LAUNFAL

The Vision of Sir Launfal, it is said, was composed almost at a single sitting. The poem shows signs of having been written rapidly. Its merits, its singleness of mood, and impetuosity of movement indicate

speed, while its metrical defects and its obscurities in
expression or design are no less significant of haste.
Of one thing we may feel sure: The haste that drove
the poem to completion was not so much the result
of a desire to have it done by a certain time, as the
impatience that springs from an author's complete
absorption in his subject — that will give him no rest
till his ideas have obtained expression.

The poem is peculiar in purpose, form, and structure. The story tells of the young knight who, before
setting out on his quest, prays for a vision to guide
him. The vision is granted. In it, he sees himself
riding out, young, hopeful, exultant in the joy of summer. At the gate of his castle a leper asks an alms.
In disgust the young knight tosses him a piece of
gold. The leper refuses the gift, for it is offered in
the wrong spirit. Then his dream changes. He sees
himself, long years after, returning in poverty and
old age, in the dead of winter, to a castle no longer
his. He is driven from its doors, and, as he sits in
the cold, the leper appears once more. Sir Launfal
has now no gold to give, but he shares with the beggar his single crust and gives him water from his
wooden bowl. Then the beggar casts off his disguise;
he is transformed into the Christ, who tells Sir Launfal that this is the true spirit of charity. It is not
what we *give*, but what we *share*, that is welcome to

the needy and of blessing to ourselves. The young knight awakens. He hangs up his armor and devotes himself to charity and hospitality. He has learned his lesson.

The structure of the poem is somewhat faulty. The Prelude has, it is true, some connection with Part First. Youth and summer are related, so are summer and warmth of heart. But Lowell seems to confound the two symbolisms. Summer is at once pride of youth that mistakes scornful bounty for true charity and the warmth of love that tries in vain to invade the castle. The rhapsody over June, notwithstanding its rare beauty, is disproportionally prominent. In the Second Part the description of winter, intended to intensify helplessness and humiliation and impressions of old age, is broken into by the description of the little brook, a description which dwells not on the desolation of winter, but on its joy and beauty.

In unity of structure, the oneness that should exist in the perfect poem, *The Vision of Sir Launfal* is deficient. But this defect is merely incidental. The beauties of the poem, however unrelated, are none the less admirable and inspiring. For while *The Vision of Sir Launfal* is a story, a story with a moral, we must not forget that it is above all a poem. It is a poem not merely because it is in verse, — that is, in rhyme and metre. Advertisements in street-

cars are often in rhyme and metre, but these are not
poetry. *The Vision of Sir Launfal* is a poem not on
account of its form but on account of its spirit. The
writer feels intensely the wonder of what he is de-
scribing and tries to make his reader feel it. The
mere story he could have told in prose. What he is
trying to tell is the magic of the summer world, the
cold, crystal beauty of winter, the sunlight that God
gives freely to us all, the mystery of human sympathy
that God would have us give and that we withhold,
all these marvels and many more he feels intensely.
And when one feels a thing so deeply that mere words
seem too bare to express it, when to these he must add
the music of metre and the link of rhyme, then he has
left the region of prose and risen into poetry.

The story is a moral story, and the moral is important; for the young Lowell was, as you have seen,
a man who took moral lessons deeply. There was
in him a mystic vein, a half belief in the direct utterance of God to men, something that made him akin to
the young knight that asks this vision from God for
his guidance. "Not what we give, but what we
share," — not what we do, but the spirit in which we
do it, — that is what tells in our own hearts in the
eye of Heaven. That is the central lesson, and this
Lowell made his own motto.

A great beauty of the poem lies in the setting, the

perfect description of a perfect day in June, and in
that contrasted description of the little brook in winter. It is these, perhaps, more than anything else, that
give the poem its greatness. We go to poetry less for
teaching than for awakening. We want the poet to
interpret to us the message of the skies, of the winds,
of the " druid woods," of the eternal sea. And of his
moral we get not a cold theological theory of life, but
a warm stirring impulse to noble action.

In studying such a poem, read it aloud. Read it
slowly, letting it, so to speak, dissolve in the mind,
till each word has given up its lesson.

Let your imagination have free wing. Do not be
afraid of enthusiasm. Let each picture call up associated recollections from your own storehouse of memory. Try to enjoy, to find the way to enjoyment. For
poetry read without pleasure is profitless.

As for the other poems included with the *Vision*,
these are not so much intended for study in themselves as for reading in connection with the chief
poem studied. For in them one finds reflected other
moods of the poet, or often the same moods, even the
same pictures in a different setting. And, by reading
them all, by laying one beside another, you will feel
emerging from them at last the man himself, a new
friend, stimulating, inspiring, speaking — though men
call him dead — to his living friends in words of noble
and uplifting significance.

BIBLIOGRAPHY

Lowell's Complete Works are published by Houghton, Mifflin, and Company. The poems and prose works can be obtained separately.

The Vision of Sir Launfal was first published in 1848. A number of editions were struck from the first plates, one appearing as late as 1875. In the collection of his poems appearing in 1857, Lowell made a number of alterations. This text gives, virtually, the final form of the poem, and is followed in this edition. It is followed also in the case of the other poems included, except in a few that appeared only in the earlier collections. Attention is called in the notes to significant variations of text in the various editions.

Biographies of Lowell have been written by E. E. Brown and by F. H. Underwood. *James Russell Lowell*, an Address by G. W. Curtis, will be found suggestive. Edward Everett Hale's *James Russell Lowell and His Friends* is full of interesting information, and has been drawn on considerably in the introduction of this volume. *Lowell's Letters*, edited by C. E. Norton, also afford much material concerning the poet's life, surroundings, and character.

In the periodicals will be found articles almost innumerable. The teacher will do well to instruct the student in the use of Poole's *Index to Periodical Literature,* which gives the title of each and the volume and page of the magazine where it is to be found. Among these is a study of the *Sir Launfal,* in *Poet-Lore,* Volume VI., p. 47. Both pupil and teacher will do well to consult it.

Studies of Lowell's work as a whole will be found in Haweis's *American Humorists,* in Richardson's *American Literature,* as well as in Nicol's, Pattee's, Paucoast's, and Matthews' works on the same subject.

Collateral reading on the subject of the days of Chivalry might take up Lanier's *Boys' King Arthur,* Scott's *Ivanhoe, The Talisman, The Abbot, The Monastery,* Tennyson's *The Idylls of the King.*

The lives of the writers with whom Lowell associated will be certain to cast some light on his own character. Some study of the beginnings of the anti-slavery agitation of New England might be taken up in this connection.

WRITERS OF LOWELL'S TIME

Bryant	1794–1878
Emerson	1803–1882
Hawthorne	1804–1864
Longfellow	1807–1882
Whittier	1807–1892
Poe	1809–1849
Holmes	1809–1894

SUBJECTS FOR COMPOSITION

1. Lowell as Patriot. In his poems, in his prose writings, in his life.
   Read, *Biglow Papers, Commemoration Ode, Political Essays*, Democracy, Article, Nation LIII., p. 56. *Lowell as Patriot.* Hale's *Lowell and His Friends. Lowell's Letters.*

2. Cambridge in the Second Quarter of the Century.
   Read, Lowell's *Cambridge Thirty Years Ago.* Hale's *Lowell, Lowell's Letters.* Magazine articles, see Poole's Index.

3. The Moral Lesson of the Poem. Compare the *Ancient Mariner*, a poem with a moral, and Poe's *Raven*, a poem without any. Should a poem necessarily teach a moral lesson? Compare pictures and music.

4. Should the Moral of a Poem be Stated. Compare the two versions of *Rhœcus*. Can a moral be implied in a story without being stated at the end? Recall cases. Which method is preferable? Why?

5. Lowell and Coleridge. The man of dreams and the man of action. Show this contrast by comparing their poems. Which has the more active teaching? Which teaches to do, which merely to feel? Apply this to the story of the lives of the men.

6. Lowell's Description of American Scenery. Was this new? What had American writers described hitherto? What English writers inspired him to describe things as he saw them?

7. Lowell's Friends. The value of association to young writers. Mention other cases. Trace the effect of literary companionship on Lowell and his friends. Read E. E. Hale's *Lowell and His Friends*.

8. American Literature and British Literature. To what extent are they one? To what extent independent and to be studied separately? Read Brander Matthews' essay, *Americanism*.

9. Original Poem. A description of spring, summer, autumn, or winter, in the same metre as *The Vision of Sir Launfal*. Do not reproduce the same scenes that Lowell describes.

10. Original Poem (or original prose story). Select appropriate title yourself. A story of feudal times, tournament, crusade, search for the Holy Grail. Read Lanier's *Boys' King Arthur; Chanson of Roland*, O'Hagan's translation; Tennyson's *Idylls of the King*.

The teacher can suggest other subjects calling for invention or comparison. It seems better to avoid subjects that call merely for research and compilation. More is gained when some creative use is made of the material collected.

LOWELL'S

THE VISION OF SIR LAUNFAL

AND OTHER POEMS

THE VISION OF SIR LAUNFAL

PRELUDE TO PART FIRST°

Over° his keys the musing organist,
  Beginning doubtfully and far away,
First lets his fingers wander as they list,
  And builds a bridge from Dreamland for his lay°:
Then, as the touch of his loved instrument
  Gives hope and fervor, nearer draws his theme,°
First guessed by faint auroral° flushes sent
  Along the wavering vista° of his dream.

———

Not only around our infancy°
Doth heaven with all its splendors lie;
Daily, with souls that cringe and plot,
We Sinais° climb and know it not.

Over our manhood bend the skies;
  Against our fallen and traitor° lives
The great winds utter prophecies°;
  With our faint hearts the mountain strives,°

B   1

Its arms outstretched, the druid° wood
    Waits with its benedicite°;
And to our age's drowsy blood
    Still shouts° the inspiring sea.   20

Earth gets its price for what Earth gives us°;
    The beggar is taxed for a corner to die in,
The priest hath his fee who comes and shrives° us,
    We bargain for the graves we lie in;
At the devil's booth° are all things sold,
Each ounce of dross costs its ounce of gold;
    For a cap and bells° our lives we pay,°
Bubbles we buy with a whole soul's tasking:
'Tis heaven alone that is given away,
'Tis only God may be had for the asking°;   30
    No price is set on the lavish summer;
    June may be had by the poorest comer.

And what is so rare as a day in June°?
    Then, if ever, come perfect days;
Then Heaven tries the earth if it be in tune,°
    And over it softly her warm ear lays:
Whether we look, or whether we listen,
We hear life murmur, or see it glisten°;
Every clod feels a stir of might,

An instinct within it that reaches and towers, 40
And, groping blindly above it for light,
  Climbs to a soul° in grass and flowers;
The flush of life° may well be seen
  Thrilling back over hills and valleys;
The cowslip startles° in meadows green,
  The buttercup catches the sun in its chalice,°
And there's never a leaf nor a blade too mean
  To be some happy creature's° palace;
The little bird sits at his door° in the sun,
  Atilt like a blossom° among the leaves, 50
And lets his illumined being o'errun
  With the deluge of summer° it receives;
His mate feels the eggs beneath her wings,
And the heart in her dumb breast flutters and sings°;
He sings to the wide world, and she to her nest,—
In the nice° ear of Nature which song is the best?

Now is the high-tide° of the year,
  And whatever of life hath ebbed away
Comes flooding back, with a ripply cheer,
  Into every bare inlet and creek and bay; 60
Now the heart is so full that a drop overfills it,
We are happy now because God wills it;
No matter how barren the past may have been,

'Tis enough for us now that the leaves are green;
We sit in the warm shade and feel right well
How the sap creeps up and the blossoms swell;
We° may shut our eyes, but we cannot help knowing
That skies are clear and grass is growing;
The breeze comes whispering in our ear,
That dandelions are blossoming near,   70
    That maize° has sprouted, that streams are flowing,
That° the river is bluer than the sky,
That the robin° is plastering his house hard by;
And if the breeze kept the good news back,
For other couriers we should not lack;
    We could guess it all by yon heifer's lowing, —
And hark! how clear bold chanticleer,°
Warmed with the new wine of the year,°
    Tells all in his lusty crowing° !

Joy comes, grief goes, we know not how;   80
Every thing is happy now,
    Every thing is upward striving;
'Tis° as easy now for the heart to be true
As for grass to be green, or skies to be blue,
    'Tis the natural way of living:
Who° knows whither the clouds have fled?
    In the unscarred heaven they leave no wake;

And the eyes forget the tears they have shed,
  And heart forgets its sorrow and ache;
The° soul partakes the season's youth,   90
  And the sulphurous rifts° of passion and woe
Lie deep 'neath a silence pure and smooth,
Like burnt-out craters healed° with snow.
What wonder if Sir Launfal° now
Remembered the keeping of his vow?

PART FIRST

I

" My golden spurs now bring to me,
  And bring to me my richest° mail,
For to-morrow I go over land and sea
  In search of the Holy Grail;
Shall never a bed for me be spread,°   100
Nor shall a pillow be under my head,
Till I begin my vow to keep;
Here on the rushes° will I sleep,
And perchance there may come a vision true
Ere day create the world anew°."
    Slowly Sir Launfal's eyes grew dim,
    Slumber fell like a cloud° on him,
And into his soul the vision flew.°

II

The° crows flapped over° by twos and threes,
  In the pool drowsed the cattle up to their knees, 110
    The little birds sang as if it were
  The one day of summer in all the year,
And the very leaves seemed to sing on the trees:
The castle° alone in the landscape lay
Like an outpost° of winter, dull and gray;
'Twas the proudest hall in the North Countree,°
And never its gates might opened be,
Save to lord or lady of high degree°;
Summer besieged it on every side,
But the churlish stone her assaults defied; 120
She could not scale° the chilly wall,
Though round it for leagues her pavilions tall
  Stretched left and right,
Over the hills and out of sight;
  Green and broad was every tent,°
  And out of each a murmur went
Till the breeze fell off° at night.

III

The drawbridge dropped with a surly clang,°
And through the dark arch° a charger° sprang,

Bearing Sir Launfal, the maiden knight,°   130
In° his gilded mail, that flamed so bright
It seemed the dark castle had gathered all
Those shafts the fierce sun had shot over its wall
  In the siege of three hundred summers long,
And, binding them all in one blazing sheaf,°
  Had cast them forth: so, young and strong,°
And lightsome as a locust-leaf,°
Sir Launfal flashed forth in his unscarred° mail,
To seek in all climes for the Holy Grail.

IV

It was morning on hill and stream and tree,°   140
  And morning in the young knight's heart;
Only the castle moodily
Rebuffed the gifts of the sunshine free,
  And gloomed by itself apart;
The season brimmed all other things up
Full as the rain fills the pitcher-plant's° cup.°

V

As Sir Launfal made morn° through the darksome gate,
  He was ware of a leper,° crouched by the same,
Who begged with his hand° and moaned as he sate;
  And a loathing over Sir Launfal came;   150

The° sunshine went out of his soul with a thrill,
   The flesh 'neath his armor 'gan shrink and crawl,
And midway its leap his heart stood still
   Like a frozen waterfall;
For this man so foul and bent of stature,°
Rasped harshly against his dainty° nature,
And seemed the one blot on the summer morn,—
So he tossed him a piece of gold in scorn.°

VI

The leper raised not the gold from the dust:
" Better to me the poor man's crust,°   160
Better the blessing of the poor,
Though I turn me empty from his door;
That is no true alms° which the hand can hold;
He gives nothing but worthless gold
   Who gives from a sense of duty;
But he who gives a slender mite,°
And gives to that which is out of sight,
   That thread of the all-sustaining Beauty°
Which runs through all and doth all unite,—
The hand cannot clasp the whole of his alms,°   170
The heart outstretches its eager palms,°
For a god° goes with it and makes it store°
To the soul that was starving in darkness before."

PRELUDE TO PART SECOND

Down° swept the chill wind from the mountain peak,°
   From the snow five thousand summers° old;
On open wold° and hill-top bleak
   It had gathered all the cold,
And whirled it like sleet° on the wanderer's cheek;
It carried a shiver everywhere°
From the unleafed° boughs and pastures bare;   180
The little brook° heard it and built a roof
'Neath which he could house him, winter-proof;
All night by the white stars' frosty gleams°
He groined° his arches and matched his beams;
Slender and clear were his crystal spars°
As the lashes of light° that trim the stars;
He sculptured every summer delight
In his halls and chambers° out of sight;
Sometimes his tinkling° waters slipt
Down through a frost-leaved forest-crypt,°   190
Long, sparkling aisles of steel-stemmed trees°
Bending to counterfeit a breeze°;
Sometimes the roof no fretwork° knew
But silvery mosses that downward grew;
Sometimes it was carved in sharp relief°

With quaint arabesques° of ice-fern leaf;
Sometimes it was simply smooth and clear
For the gladness of heaven° to shine through, and here
He had caught the nodding bulrush-tops
And hung them thickly with diamond drops,   200
That crystalled the beams° of moon and sun,
And made a star of every one:
No mortal builder's most rare device
Could match this winter-palace° of ice;
'Twas° as if every image that mirrored lay
In his depths serene through the summer day,
Each fleeting shadow of earth and sky,
    Lest the happy model should be lost,
Had been mimicked in fairy masonry
    By the elfin builders of the frost.   210

Within the hall° are song and laughter,
    The cheeks of Christmas° glow red and jolly,
And sprouting is every corbel° and rafter
With lightsome° green of ivy and holly;
Through the deep gulf° of the chimney wide
Wallows the Yule-log's° roaring tide;
The broad flame-pennons droop° and flap
    And belly and tug as a flag in the wind;
Like a locust shrills the imprisoned sap,

Hunted to death° in its galleries blind;   220
And swift little troops of silent sparks,
    Now pausing, now scattering away as in fear,
Go threading the soot-forest's° tangled darks,
    Like herds of startled deer.°

But the wind without was eager and sharp,
Of Sir Launfal's gray hair it makes a harp,
        And rattles and wrings°
        The icy strings,°
    Singing, in dreary monotone,
    A Christmas carol° of its own,   230
    Whose burden still, as he might guess,
    Was — "Shelterless, shelterless, shelterless!"

The voice of the seneschal° flared like a torch°
As he shouted the wanderer away from the porch,
And he sat in the gateway° and saw all night
    The great hall-fire, so cheery and bold,
    Through the window-slits° of the castle old,
Build out its piers° of ruddy light
    Against the drift° of the cold.

PART SECOND

I

THERE was never a leaf on bush or tree,   240
The bare boughs rattled shudderingly;
The river was numb and could not speak,
   For the weaver Winter° its shroud had spun;
A single crow on the tree-top bleak
   From his shining feathers shed off° the cold sun.
Again it was morning, but shrunk and cold,
As if her veins were sapless and old,
And she rose up decrepitly
For a last dim look at earth and sea.

II

Sir Launfal turned from his own hard gate,°   250
For another heir in his earldom° sate;
An old, bent man, worn out and frail,
He came back from seeking the Holy Grail;
Little he recked of his earldom's loss,
No more on his surcoat° was blazoned° the cross,
But deep in his soul the sign° he wore,
The badge of the suffering and the poor.

III

Sir Launfal's raiment thin and spare
Was idle mail° 'gainst the barbèd° air,
For it was just at the Christmas time;   260
So he mused, as he sat, of a sunnier clime,
And sought for a shelter from cold and snow
In the light and warmth of long ago;
He sees the snake-like° caravan crawl
O'er the edge of the desert, black and small,
Then nearer and nearer, till, one by one,
He can count the camels in the sun,
As over the red-hot sands they pass
To where, in its slender necklace of grass,
The little spring laughed and leapt in the shade,°   270
And with its own self like an infant played,
And waved its signal of palms.°

IV

"For° Christ's sweet sake, I beg an alms;°"
The happy° camels may reach the spring,
But Sir Launfal sees only the gruesome thing,
The leper, lank as the rain-blanched bone,
That cowers beside him, a thing as lone
And white° as the ice-isles of Northern seas
In the desolate horror of his disease.

V

And Sir Launfal said, — "I behold in thee   280
An image of Him who died on the tree° ;
Thou also hast had thy crown of thorns,° —
Thou also hast had the world's buffets and scorns, —
And to thy life were not denied
The wounds° in the hands and feet and side ;
Mild Mary's Son, acknowledge me ;
Behold, through him, I give to thee° ! "

VI

Then the soul of the leper stood up in his eyes°
    And looked at Sir Launfal, and straightway he
Remembered in what a haughtier guise°   290
    He had flung an alms to leprosie,°
When he girt° his young life up in gilded mail
And set forth in search of the Holy Grail.
The heart within him was ashes and dust° ;
He parted in twain his single crust,
He broke the ice on the streamlet's brink,
And gave the leper to eat and drink ;
'Twas a mouldy crust of coarse brown bread,
    'Twas water out of a wooden bowl, —
Yet with fine wheaten bread° was the leper fed,   300
    And 'twas red wine he drank with his thirsty soul.°

VII

As Sir Launfal mused° with a downcast face,
A light shone round about the place;
The leper no longer crouched at his side,
But stood before him glorified,°
Shining and tall and fair and straight
As the pillar that stood by the Beautiful Gate,° —
Himself the Gate° whereby men can
Enter the temple of God in Man.   309

VIII

His words were shed softer than leaves° from the pine,
And they fell on Sir Launfal as snows on the brine,
Which mingle their softness and quiet in one
With the shaggy unrest° they float down upon;
And the voice that was calmer than silence° said,
"Lo, it is I, be not afraid!
In many climes, without avail,
Thou hast spent thy life for the Holy Grail;
Behold, it is here, — this cup which thou
Didst fill at the streamlet for me but now;
This crust is my body broken for thee,   320
This water His blood that died on the tree;
The Holy Supper is kept, indeed,
In whatso we share with another's need, —

Not what we give, but what we share, —
For the gift without the giver is bare ;
Who gives himself with his alms feeds three, —
Himself, his hungering neighbor, and me."

IX

Sir Launfal awoke,° as from a swound° ; —
"The Grail in my castle here° is found !
Hang my idle armor up on the wall,   330
Let it be the spider's banquet-hall ;
He must be fenced with stronger mail°
Who would seek and find the Holy Grail."

X

The castle-gate stands open now,
    And the wanderer is welcome to the hall
As the hangbird° is to the elm-tree bough ;
    No longer scowl the turrets tall,
The Summer's long siege° at last is o'er ;
When the first poor outcast went in at the door,
She entered with him in disguise,   340
And mastered the fortress by surprise ;
There is no spot she loves so well on ground,
She lingers and smiles there the whole year round° ;

The meanest serf° on Sir Launfal's land
Has hall and bower° at his command;
And there's no poor man in the North Countree°
But is lord of the earldom as much as he.

C

AN INDIAN SUMMER° REVERIE

WHAT visionary tints the year puts on,
When falling leaves falter through motionless air°
    Or numbly cling and shiver to be gone!
How shimmer the low flats and pastures bare,
    As with her nectar Hebe Autumn° fills
    The bowl between me and those distant hills.
And smiles and shakes abroad her misty, tremulous hair!

No more the landscape holds its wealth apart,
Making me poorer in my poverty,
    But mingles with my senses and my heart;   10
My own projected spirit° seems to me
    In her own reverie the world to steep°;
    'Tis she that waves to sympathetic sleep,
Moving, as she is moved, each field and hill and tree.

How fuse and mix, with what unfelt degrees,
Clasped by the faint horizon's languid arms,
    Each into each, the hazy distances!

The softened season all the landscape charms;
　　Those hills, my native village that embay,
　　In waves of dreamier purple roll away, '　　20
And floating in mirage seem all the glimmering farms.

　　Far distant sounds the hidden chickadee
　Close at my side; far distant sound the leaves;
　　The fields seem fields of dream, where Memory
　Wanders like gleaning Ruth°; and as the sheaves
　　Of wheat and barley wavered in the eye
　　Of Boaz as the maiden's glow went by,
So tremble and seem remote all things the sense receives.

　　The cock's shrill trump, that tells of scattered corn,
　Passed breezily on by all his flapping mates,　　30
　　Faint and more faint, from barn to barn is borne,
　Southward, perhaps to far Magellan's Straits°;
　　Dimly I catch the throb of distant flails;
　　Silently overhead the henhawk sails,
With watchful, measuring eye, and for his quarry°
　　waits.

　　The sobered robin, hunger-silent now,
　Seeks cedar-berries blue, his autumn cheer;

The squirrel, on the shingly shagbark's bough,
Now saws, now lists with downward eye and ear,
  Then drops his nut, and, with a chipping bound, 40
  Whisks to his winding fastness underground;
The clouds like swans drift down the streaming atmos-
    phere.

O'er yon bare knoll the pointed cedar shadows
Drowse on the crisp, gray moss; the ploughman's
    call
  Creeps faint as smoke from black, fresh-furrowed
    meadows;
  The single crow a single caw lets fall;
  And all around me every bush and tree
  Says Autumn's here, and Winter soon will be,
Who snows his soft, white sleep and silence over all.

The birch, most shy and lady-like of trees,°   50
Her poverty, as best she may, retrieves,
  And hints at her foregone gentilities
With some saved relics of her wealth of leaves;
  The swamp-oak, with his royal purple on,
  Glares red as blood across the sinking sun,
As one who proudlier to a falling fortune cleaves.

He looks a sachem, in red blanket wrapt,
Who, 'mid some council of the sad-garbed° whites,
  Erect and stern, in his own memories lapt,
With distant eye broods over other sights,   60
  Sees the hushed wood the city's flare replace,
  The wounded turf heal o'er the railway's trace,
And roams the savage Past of his undwindled rights.°

The red-oak, softer-grained, yields all for lost,
And, with his crumpled foliage stiff and dry,
  After the first betrayal of the frost,
Rebuffs the kiss of the relenting sky;
  The chestnuts, lavish of their long-hid gold,
  To the faint Summer, beggared now and old,
Pour back the sunshine hoarded 'neath her favoring
      eye.   70

The ash her purple drops forgivingly
And sadly, breaking not the general hush;
  The maple-swamps glow like a sunset sea,
Each leaf a ripple with its separate flush;
  All round the wood's edge creeps the skirting
      blaze
  Of bushes low, as when, on cloudy days,
Ere the rain falls, the cautious farmer burns his brush.

O'er yon low wall, which guards one unkempt
    zone,
Where vines and weeds and scrub-oaks intertwine
    Safe from the plough, whose° rough, discordant
      stone   80
Is massed to one soft gray by lichens fine,
    The tangled blackberry, crossed and recrossed,
      weaves
    A prickly network of ensanguined leaves;
Hard by, with coral beads, the prim black-alders shine.

Pillaring with flame this crumbling boundary,
    Whose loose blocks topple 'neath the ploughboy's
      foot,
    Who, with each sense shut fast except the eye,
Creeps close and scares the jay he hoped to shoot,
    The woodbine up the elm's straight stem aspires,
    Coiling it, harmless, with autumnal fires;   90
In the ivy's paler blaze the martyr° oak stands mute.

Below, the Charles — a stripe of nether sky,
    Now hid by rounded apple trees between,
    Whose gaps the misplaced° sail sweeps bellying
      by,

Now flickering golden through a woodland screen,
  Then spreading out, at his next turn beyond,
  A silver circle, like an inland pond —
Slips seaward, silently, through marshes purple and
  green.

Dear marshes! vain to him the gift of sight
Who cannot in their various incomes share,   100
  From every season drawn, of shade and light,
Who sees in them but levels brown and bare;
  Each change of storm or sunshine scatters free
  On them its largess of variety,
For Nature with cheap means still works her wonders
  rare.°

In Spring they lie one broad expanse of green,
  O'er which the light winds run with glimmering
  feet;
  Here, yellower stripes track out the creek unseen,
There, darker growths o'er hidden ditches meet:
  And purpler stains show where the blossoms
  crowd,   110
  As if the silent shadow of a cloud
Hung there becalmed, with the next breath to fleet.

All round, upon the river's slippery edge,
Witching to deeper calm the drowsy tide,
  Whispers and leans the breeze-entangling sedge;
Through emerald glooms the lingering waters slide,
  Or, sometimes wavering, throw back the sun,
  And the stiff banks in eddies melt and run
Of dimpling light, and with the current seem to glide.

In Summer 'tis a blithesome sight to see,   120
As, step by step, with measured swing, they pass,
  The wide-ranked mowers wading to the knee,
Their sharp scythes panting through the thickset
    grass ;
  Then, stretched beneath a rick's shade in a ring,
  Their nooning take, while one begins to sing
A stave that droops and dies 'neath the close sky of
    brass.

Meanwhile that devil-may-care, the bobolink,
Remembering duty, in mid-quaver stops
  Just ere he sweeps o'er rapture's tremulous brink,
And 'twixt the winrows most demurely drops,   130
  A decorous bird of business, who provides
  For his brown mate and fledglings six besides,
And looks from right to left, a farmer 'mid his crops.

Another change subdues them in the Fall,
But saddens not; they still show merrier tints,
 Though sober russet seems to cover all;
When the first sunshine through their dew-drops
  glints,
 Look how the yellow clearness, streamed across,
 Redeems with rarer hues the season's loss,
As Dawn's feet there had touched and left their rosy
  prints.   140

Or come when sunset gives its freshened zest,
Lean o'er the bridge and let the ruddy thrill,
 While the shorn sun swells° down the hazy west,
Glow opposite; — the marshes drink their fill
 And swoon with purple veins, then slowly fade
 Through pink to brown, as eastward moves the
  shade,
Lengthening with stealthy creep, of Simond's darken-
  ing hill.

Later, and yet ere Winter wholly shuts,
Ere through the first dry snow the runner grates,
 And the loath cart-wheel screams in slippery
  ruts,   150
While firmer ice the eager boy awaits,°

Trying each buckle and strap beside the fire,
  And until bed-time plays with his desire,
Twenty times putting on and off his new-bought
      skates; —

    Then, every morn, the river's banks shine bright
  With smooth plate-armor,° treacherous and frail,
    By the frost's clinking hammers forged at night,
  'Gainst which the lances of the sun prevail,
      Giving a pretty emblem of the day
      When guiltier arms in light shall melt away,° 160
And states shall move free-limbed, loosed from war's
      cramping mail.°

    And now those waterfalls° the ebbing river
  Twice every day creates on either side
      Tinkle, as through their fresh-sparred grots° they
        shiver
  In grass-arched channels to the sun denied;
      High flaps in sparkling blue the far-heard crow,
      The silvered flats gleam frostily below,
Suddenly drops the gull and breaks the glassy tide.

    But, crowned in turn by vying seasons three,
  Their winter halo hath a fuller ring;   170
      This glory seems to rest immovably, —

The others were too fleet and vanishing;
　　When the hid tide is at its highest flow,
　　O'er marsh and stream one breathless trance of
　　　snow
With brooding fulness awes and hushes every thing.

　　The sunshine seems blown off by the bleak wind,°
As pale as formal candles lit by day;
　　Gropes to the sea the river dumb and blind;
The brown ricks, snow-thatched by the storm in
　　play,
　　Show pearly breakers° combing o'er their lea,　180
　　White crests as of some just enchanted sea,
Checked in their maddest leap and hanging poised
　　midway.

　　But when the eastern blow, with rain aslant,
From mid-sea's prairies green and rolling plains
　　Drives in his wallowing herds of billows gaunt,
And the roused Charles remembers in his veins
　　Old Ocean's blood and snaps his gyves of frost,
　　That tyrannous silence° on the shores is tost
In dreary wreck, and crumbling desolation reigns.

　　Edgewise or flat, in Druid-like° device,　　　190
　　With leaden pools between or gullies bare,

The blocks lie strewn, a bleak Stonehenge° of ice;
No life, no sound, to break the grim despair,
Save sullen plunge, as through the sedges stiff
Down crackles riverward some thaw-sapped cliff,
Or when the close-wedged fields of ice crunch here
and there.

But let me turn from fancy-pictured scenes
To that whose pastoral calm before me lies:
Here nothing harsh or rugged intervenes;
The early evening with her misty dyes   200
Smooths off the ravelled edges of the nigh,
Relieves the distant with her cooler sky,
And tones the landscape down, and soothes the wearied
eyes.

There gleams my native village, dear to me,
Though higher change's waves each day are seen,
Whelming fields famed in boyhood's history,
Sanding with houses the diminished green;
There, in red brick, which softening time defies,
Stand square and stiff the Muses' factories°; —
How with my life knit up is every well-known
scene!   210

Flow on, dear river! not alone you flow
To outward sight, and through your marshes wind;
  Fed from the mystic springs of long-ago,
Your twin flows silent through my world of mind:
  Grow dim, dear marshes, in the evening's gray!
  Before my inner sight ye stretch away,
And will for ever, though these fleshly eyes grow blind.

Beyond the hillock's house bespotted swell,°
Where Gothic chapels° house the horse and chaise,
  Where quiet cits in Grecian temples dwell,   220
Where Coptic tombs° resound with prayer and
    praise,
  Where dust and mud the equal year divide,
  There gentle Allston° lived, and wrought, and died,
Transfiguring street and shop with his illumined gaze.

Virgilium vidi tantum, — I have seen
But as a boy, who looks alike on all,
  That misty hair, that fine Undine-like mien,°
Tremulous as down° to feeling's faintest call; —
  Ah, dear old homestead°! count it to thy fame
  That thither many times the Painter came; — 230
One elm yet bears his name, a feathery tree and tall.

Swiftly the present fades in memory's glow, —
Our only sure possession is the past;
    The village blacksmith° died a month ago,
And dim to me the forge's roaring blast;
    Soon fire-new mediævals° we shall see
    Oust the black smithy from its chestnut tree,
And that hewn down, perhaps, the bee-hive green and
    vast.

How many times, prouder than king on throne,
    Loosed from the village school-dame's A-s and B-s, 240
Panting have I the creaky bellows blown,
And watched the pent volcano's red increase,°
    Then paused to see the ponderous sledge, brought
        down
    By that hard arm voluminous and brown,
From the white iron swarm° its golden vanishing bees.

Dear native town! whose choking elms each year
With eddying dust before their time turn gray,
    Pining for rain, — to me thy dust is dear;
It glorifies the eve of summer day,
    And when the westering sun half-sunken burns, 250
    The mote-thick air to deepest orange turns,
The westward horseman rides through clouds of gold
    away.

So palpable, I've seen those unshorn few,
The six old willows° at the causey's end,
  (Such trees Paul Potter° never dreamed nor drew),
Through this dry mist their checkering shadows
    send,
    Striped, here and there, with many a long-drawn
      thread,
    Where streamed through leafy chinks the trem-
      bling red,
Past which, in one bright trail, the hangbird's flashes
  blend.

Yes, dearer for thy dust than all that e'er,   260
Beneath the awarded crown of victory,
  Gilded the blown Olympic charioteer;
Though lightly prized the ribboned parchments
    three,
    Yet *collegisse juvat*° I am glad
    That here what colleging was mine I had, —
It linked another tie, dear native town, with thee!

Nearer art thou than simply native earth,
My dust with thine concedes a deeper tie;
  A closer claim thy soil may well put forth,
Something of kindred more than sympathy;   270

For in thy bounds I reverently° laid away
That blinding anguish of forsaken clay,
That title I seemed to have in earth and sea and sky,

That portion of my life more choice to me°
(Though brief, yet in itself so round and whole)
Than all the imperfect residue can be; —
The Artist saw his statue of the soul
Was perfect; so, with one regretful stroke,
The earthen model into fragments broke,
And without her the impoverished seasons roll.   280

RHŒCUS

God sends his teachers unto every age,
To every clime, and every race of men,
With revelations fitted to their growth
And shape of mind, nor gives the realm of Truth
Into the selfish rule of one sole race:
Therefore each form of worship that hath swayed
The life of man, and given it to grasp
The master-key of knowledge, reverence,
Enfolds some germs of goodness and of right;
Else never had the eager soul, which loathes   10
The slothful down of pampered ignorance,
Found in it even a moment's fitful rest.

There is an instinct in the human heart
Which makes that all the fables it hath coined,
To justify the reign of its belief
And strengthen it by beauty's right divine,
Veil in their inner cells a mystic gift,
Which, like the hazel twig, in faithful hands,
Points surely to the hidden springs of truth.

D

For, as in nature naught is made in vain,   20
But all things have within their hull of use
A wisdom and a meaning which may speak
Of spiritual secrets to the ear
Of spirit; so, in whatsoe'er the heart
Hath fashioned for a solace to itself,
To make its inspirations suit its creed,
And from the niggard hands of falsehood wring
Its needful food of truth, there ever is
A sympathy with Nature, which reveals,
Not less than her own works, pure gleams of light   30
And earnest parables of inward lore.
Hear now this fairy legend of old Greece,
As full of freedom, youth, and beauty still
As the immortal freshness of that grace
Carved for all ages on some Attic frieze.

    A youth named Rhœcus, wandering in the wood,
Saw an old oak just trembling to its fall,
And, feeling pity of so fair a tree,
He propped its gray trunk with admiring care,
And with a thoughtless footstep loitered on.   40
But, as he turned, he heard a voice behind
That murmured " Rhœcus ! "   'Twas as if the leaves,
Stirred by a passing breath, had murmured it.

And, while he paused bewildered, yet again
It murmured "Rhœcus!" softer than a breeze.
He started and beheld with dizzy eyes
What seemed the substance of a happy dream
Stand there before him, spreading a warm glow
Within the green glooms of the shadowy oak.
It seemed a woman's shape, yet all too fair   50
To be a woman, and with eyes too meek
For any that were wont to mate with gods.
All naked like a goddess stood she there,
And like a goddess all too beautiful
To feel the guilt-born earthliness of shame.
"Rhœcus, I am the Dryad° of this tree,"
Thus she began, dropping her low-toned words
Serene, and full, and clear, as drops of dew,
"And with it I am doomed to live and die;
The rain and sunshine are my caterers,   60
Nor have I other bliss than simple life;
Now ask me what thou wilt, that I can give,
And with a thankful joy it shall be thine."

Then Rhœcus, with a flutter at the heart,
Yet, by the prompting of such beauty, bold,
Answered: "What is there that can satisfy
The endless craving of the soul but love?

Give me thy love, or but the hope of that
Which must be evermore my spirit's goal."
After a little pause she said again,   70
But with a glimpse of sadness in her tone,
"I give it, Rhœcus, though a perilous gift;
An hour before the sunset meet me here."
And straightway there was nothing he could see
But the green glooms beneath the shadowy oak,
And not a sound came to his straining ears
But the low trickling rustle of the leaves,
And far away upon an emerald slope
The falter of an idle shepherd's pipe.

Now, in those days of simpleness and faith,   80
Men did not think that happy things were dreams
Because they overstepped the narrow bourne
Of likelihood, but reverently deemed
Nothing too wondrous or too beautiful
To be the guerdon of a daring heart.
So Rhœcus made no doubt that he was blest,
And all along unto the city's gate
Earth seemed to spring beneath him as he walked,
The clear, broad sky looked bluer than its wont,
And he could scarce believe he had not wings,   90
Such sunshine seemed to glitter through his veins
Instead of blood, so light he felt and strange.

Young Rhœcus had a faithful heart enough,
But one that in the present dwelt too much
And, taking with blithe welcome whatsoe'er
Chance gave of joy, was wholly bound in that,
Like the contented peasant of a vale,
Deemed it the world, and never looked beyond.
So, haply meeting in the afternoon
Some comrades who were playing at the dice,   100
He joined them and forgot all else beside.

The dice were rattling at the merriest,
And Rhœcus, who had met but sorry luck,
Just laughed in triumph at a happy throw,
When through the room there hummed a yellow bee
That buzzed about his ear with down-dropped legs
As if too light.   And Rhœcus laughed and said,
Feeling how red and flushed he was with loss,
"By Venus! does he take me for a rose?"
And brushed him off with rough, impatient hand.   110
But still the bee came back, and thrice again
Rhœcus did beat him off with growing wrath.
Then through the window flew the wounded bee,
And Rhœcus, tracking him with angry eyes,
Saw a sharp mountain-peak of Thessaly
Against the red disk of the setting sun, —

And instantly the blood sank from his heart,
As if its very walls had caved away.
Without a word he turned, and, rushing forth,
Ran madly through the city and the gate,   120
And o'er the plain which now the wood's long shade,
By the low sun thrown forward broad and dim,
Darkened well-nigh unto the city's wall.

Quite spent and out of breath he reached the tree,
And, listening fearfully, he heard once more
The low voice murmur "Rhœcus!" close at hand:
Whereat he looked around him, but could see
Naught but the deepening glooms beneath the oak.
Then sighed the voice, "O Rhœcus! nevermore
Shalt thou behold me or by day or night,   130
Me, who would fain have blessed thee with a love
More ripe and bounteous than ever yet
Filled up with nectar any mortal heart:
But thou didst scorn my humble messenger,
And send'st him back to me with bruisèd wings.
We spirits only show to gentle eyes.
We ever ask an undivided love,
And he who scorns the least of nature's works
Is thenceforth exiled and shut out from all.
Farewell! for thou canst never see me more."   140

Then Rhœcus beat his breast, and groaned aloud,
And cried, "Be pitiful! forgive me yet
This once, and I shall never need it more!"
"Alas!" the voice returned, "'tis thou art blind,
Not I unmerciful; I can forgive,
But have no skill to heal thy spirit's eyes;
Only the soul hath power o'er itself." °
With that again there murmured "Nevermore!"
And Rhœcus after heard no other sound,
Except the rattling of the oak's crisp leaves,   150
Like the long surf upon a distant shore,
Raking the sea-worn pebbles up and down.
The night had gathered round him : o'er the plain
The city sparkled with its thousand lights,
And sounds of revel fell upon his ear
Harshly and like a curse; above, the sky,
With all its bright sublimity of stars,
Deepened, and on his forehead smote the breeze :
Beauty was all around him and delight,
But from that eve he was alone on earth.   160

THE BOBOLINK

'Ανήριθμον γέλασμα°

ANACREON° of the meadow,
Drunk with the joy of spring!
Beneath the tall pine's voiceful shadow
I lie and drink thy jargoning;
My soul is full with melodies,
One drop would overflow it,
And send the tears into mine eyes, —
But what carest thou to know it?
Thy heart is free as mountain air,
And of thy lays thou hast no care,   10
Scattering them gayly everywhere,
Happy, unconscious poet!

Upon a tuft of meadow grass,
While thy loved-one° tends the nest,
Thou swayest as the breezes pass,
Unburdening thy o'erfull breast
Of the crowded songs that fill it,
Just as joy may choose to will it.

Lord of thy love and liberty,
The blithest bird of merry May,   20
Thou turnest thy bright eyes on me,
That say as plain as eye can say, —
" Here sit we, here in the summer weather,
I and my modest mate together;
Whatever your wise thoughts may be,
Under that gloomy old pine-tree,
We do not value them a feather."

Now, leaving earth and me behind,
Thou beatest up against the wind,
Or, floating slowly down before it,   30
Above thy grass-hid nest thou flutterest
And thy bridal love-song utterest,
Raining showers of music o'er it.
Weary never, still thou trillest
Spring-gladsome lays,
As of moss-rimmed water-brooks
Murmuring through pebbly nooks
In quiet summer days.
My heart with happiness thou fillest,
I seem again to be a boy°   40
Watching thee, gay, blithesome lover,
O'er the bending grass-tops hover,

Quivering thy wings for joy.
There's something in the apple-blossom,
The greening grass and bobolink's song,
That wakes again within my bosom
Feelings which have slumbered long.
As long, long years ago I wandered,
I seem to wander even yet,
The hours the idle school-boy squandered,   50
The man would die ere he'd forget.
O hours that frosty eld deemed wasted,
Nodding his gray head toward my books,
I dearer prize the lore I tasted
With you, among the trees and brooks,
Than all that I have gained since then
From learnèd books or study-withered men!
Nature, thy soul was one with mine,
And, as a sister by a younger brother
Is loved, each flowing to the other,   60
Such love for me was thine.
Or wert thou not more like a loving mother
With sympathy and loving power to heal,
Against whose heart my throbbing head I'd lay
And moan my childish sorrows all away,
Till calm and holiness would o'er me steal?
Was not the golden sunset a dear friend?

Found I no kindness in the silent moon,
And the green trees, whose tops did sway and bend,
Low singing evermore their pleasant tune ?   70
Felt I no heart in dim and solemn woods —
No loved-one's voice in lonely solitudes ?
Yes, yes ! unhoodwinked then my spirit's eyes,
Blind leader had not *taught* me to be wise.

  Dear hours ! which now again I overlive,
Hearing and seeing with the ears and eyes
Of childhood, ye were bees, that to the hive
Of my young heart came laden with rich prize,
Gathered in fields and woods and sunny dells, to be
My spirit's food in days more wintery.   80
Yea, yet again ye come ! ye come !
And like a child once more at home
After long sojourning in alien climes,
I lie upon my mother's breast,
Feeling the blessedness of rest,
And dwelling in the light of other times.

O ye whose living is not *Life*,
Whose dying is but death,
Song, empty toil and petty strife,
Rounded with loss of breath !   90

Go, look on Nature's countenance,
Drink in the blessings of her glance;
Look on the sunset, hear the wind,
The cataract, the awful thunder;
Go, worship by the sea;
Then, and then only, shall ye find,
With ever-growing wonder,
Man is not all in all to ye;
Go with a meek and humble soul,
Then shall the scales of self unroll   100
From off your eyes, — the weary packs
Drop from your heavy-laden backs;
And ye shall see,
With reverent and hopeful eyes,
Glowing with new-born energies,
How great a thing it is to BE!

TO THE DANDELION

DEAR common flower, that grow'st beside the way,
Fringing the dusty road with harmless gold,
   First pledge of blithesome May,
Which children pluck, and, full of pride, uphold,
High-hearted buccaneers, o'erjoyed that they
An Eldorado° in the grass have found,
   Which not the rich earth's ample round
May match in wealth, — thou art more dear to me
Than all the prouder summer-blooms may be.

  Gold such as thine ne'er drew the Spanish prow   10
Through the primeval hush of Indian seas,
   Nor wrinkled the lean brow
Of age, to rob the lover's heart of ease;
'Tis the spring's largess, which she scatters now
To rich and poor alike, with lavish hand,
   Though most hearts never understand
To take it at God's value, but pass by
The offered wealth with unrewarded eye.

Thou art my tropics and mine Italy;
To look at thee unlocks a warmer clime;   20
   The eyes thou givest me
Are in the heart, and heed not space or time:
Not in mid June the golden-cuirassed bee
Feels a more summer-like, warm ravishment
   In the white lily's breezy tent,
His fragrant Sybaris,° than I, when first
From the dark green thy yellow circles burst.

Then think I of deep shadows on the grass, —
Of meadows where in sun the cattle graze,
   Where, as the breezes pass,   30
The gleaming rushes lean a thousand ways, —
Of leaves that slumber in a cloudy mass,
Or whiten in the wind, — of waters blue
   That from the distance sparkle through
Some woodland gap, — and of a sky above
Where one white cloud like a stray lamb doth move.

My childhood's earliest thoughts are linked with
   thee;
The sight of thee calls back the robin's song,
   Who, from the dark old tree
Beside the door, sang clearly all day long,   40

And I, secure in childish piety,
Listened as if I heard an angel sing
   With news from heaven, which he could bring
Fresh every day to my untainted ears,
When birds and flowers and I were happy peers.

   How like a prodigal doth nature seem,
When thou, for all thy gold, so common art!
   Thou teachest me to deem
More sacredly of every human heart,
Since each reflects in joy its scanty gleam 50
Of Heaven, and could some wondrous secret show,
   Did we but pay the love we owe,
And with a child's undoubting wisdom look
On all these living pages of God's book.

AN INCIDENT IN A RAILROAD CAR°

HE spoke of Burns: men rude and rough
    Pressed round to hear the praise of one
Whose heart was made of manly, simple stuff,
    As homespun as their own.

And, when he read, they forward leaned
    Drinking with eager hearts and ears,
His brook-like songs whom glory never weaned
    From humble smiles and tears.

Slowly there grew a tender awe,
    Sunlike, o'er faces brown and hard,   10
As if in him who read they felt and saw
    Some presence of the bard.

It was a sight for sin and wrong
    And slavish tyranny to see,
A sight to make our faith more pure and strong
    In high humanity.

I thought, these men will carry hence
   Promptings their former life above,
And something of a finer reverence
   For beauty, truth, and love.   20

God scatters love on every side,
   Freely among his children all,
And always hearts are lying open wid
   Wherein some grains may fall.

There is no wind but soweth seeds
   Of a more true and open life,
Which burst, unlooked for, into high-souled deeds,
   With wayside beauty rife.

We find within these souls of ours
   Some wild germs of a higher birth,   30
Which in the poet's tropic heart bear flowers
   Whose fragrance fills the earth.

Within the hearts of all men lie
   These promises of wider bliss,
Which blossom into hopes that cannot die,
   In sunny hours like this.

   E

All that hath been majestical
    In life or death, since time began,
Is native in the simple heart of all,
    The angel heart of man.   40

And thus, among the untaught poor
    Great deeds and feelings find a home,
Which casts in shadow all the golden lore
    Of classic Greece or Rome.

O, mighty brother-soul of man,
    Where'er thou art, in low or high,
Thy skiey arches with exulting span
    O'er-roof infinity!

All thoughts that mould the age begin
    Deep down within the primitive soul,
And from the many slowly upward win   50
    To one who grasps the whole.

In his wide brain the feeling deep
    Which struggled on the many's tongue
Swells to a tide of thought, whose surges leap
    O'er the weak thrones of wrong.

All thought begins in feeling, — wide
   In the great mass its base is hid,
And, narrowing up to thought, stands glorified,
   A moveless pyramid.   60

Nor is he far astray who deems
   That every hope, which rises and grows broad
In the world's heart by ordered impulse streams
   From the great heart of God.

God wills, man hopes; in common souls
   Hope is but vague and undefined,
Till from the poet's tongue the message rolls
   A blessing to his kind.

Never did Poesy appear
   So full of heav'n to me, as when   70
I saw how it would pierce through pride and fear,
   To the lives of coarsest men.

It may be glorious to write
   Thoughts that shall glad the two or three
High souls like those far stars that come in sight
   Once in a century; —

But better far it is to speak
  One simple word, which now and then
Shall waken their free nature in the weak
  And friendless sons of men;   80

To write some earnest verse or line
  Which, seeking not the praise of art,
Shall make a clearer faith and manhood shine
  In the untutored heart.

He who doth this, in verse or prose,
  May be forgotten in his day,
But surely shall be crowned at last with those
  Who live and speak for aye.

LINES°

SUGGESTED BY THE GRAVES OF TWO ENGLISH SOLDIERS
ON CONCORD BATTLE-GROUND

THE same good blood that now refills
    The dotard Orient's shrunken veins,
The same whose vigor westward thrills,
    Bursting Nevada's silver chains,
Poured here upon the April grass,
    Freckled with red the herbage new;
On reeled the battle's trampling mass,
    Back to the ash the bluebird flew.

Poured here in vain; — that sturdy blood
    Was meant to make the earth more green, —   10
But in a higher, gentler mood
    Than broke this April noon serene;
Two graves are here; to mark the place,
    At head and foot, an unhewn stone,
O'er which the herald lichens trace
    The blazon of Oblivion.

These men were brave enough, and true
    To the hired soldier's bull-dog creed;
What brought them here they never knew,
    They fought as suits the English breed;   20
They came three thousand miles, and died,
    To keep the Past upon its throne;
Unheard, beyond the ocean tide,
    Their English mother made her moan.

The turf that covers them no thrill
    Sends up to fire the heart and brain;
No stronger purpose nerves the will,
    No hope renews its youth again:
From farm to farm the Concord glides,
    And trails my fancy with its flow;   30
O'erhead the balanced henhawk slides,
    Twinned in the river's heaven below.

But go, whose Bay State bosom stirs,
    Proud of thy birth and neighbor's right,
Where sleep the heroic villagers
    Borne red and stiff from Concord fight;
Thought Reuben, snatching down his gun,
    Or Seth, as ebbed the life away,
What earthquake rifts would shoot and run
    World-wide from that short April fray?   40

What then?   With heart and hand they wrought,
　　According to their village light;
'Twas for the Future that they fought
　　Their rustic faith in what was right.
Upon earth's tragic stage they burst
　　Unsummoned, in the humble sock;
Theirs the fifth act; the curtain first
　　Rose long ago on Charles's block.

Their graves have voices; if they threw
　　Dice charged with fates beyond their ken,   50
Yet to their instincts they were true,
　　And had the genius to be men.
Fine privilege of Freedom's host,
　　Of even foot-soldiers for the Right! —
For centuries dead, ye are not lost,
　　Your graves send courage forth, and might.

THE SHEPHERD OF KING ADMETUS°

THERE came a youth upon the earth,
  Some thousand years ago,
Whose slender hands were nothing worth,
Whether to plough, or reap, or sow.

Upon an empty tortoise-shell
  He stretched some chords, and drew
Music that made men's bosoms swell
Fearless, or brimmed their eyes with dew.

But King Admetus, one who had
  Pure taste by right divine,   10
Decreed his singing not too bad
To hear between the cups of wine:

And so, well pleased with being soothed
  Into a sweet half-sleep,
Three times his kingly beard he smoothed,
And made him viceroy o'er his sheep.

His words were simple words enough,
   And yet he used them so,
That what in other mouths was rough
In his seemed musical and low.   20

Men called him but a shiftless youth,
   In whom no good they saw;
And yet, unwittingly, in truth,
They made his careless words their law.

They knew not how he learned at all,
   For idly, hour by hour,
He sat and watched the dead leaves fall,
Or mused upon a common flower.

It seemed the loveliness of things
   Did teach him all their use,   30
For, in mere weeds, and stones, and springs,
He found a healing power profuse.

Men granted that his speech was wise,
   But, when a glance they caught
Of his slim grace and woman's eyes,
They laughed, and called him good-for-naught.

Yet after he was dead and gone,
   And e'en his memory dim,
Earth seemed more sweet to live upon,
More full of love, because of him.   40

And day by day more holy grew
   Each spot where he had trod,
Till after-poets only knew
Their first-born brother as a god.

THE BEGGAR°

A BEGGAR through the world am I,
From place to place I wander by.
Fill up my pilgrim's scrip for me,
For Christ's sweet sake and charity!

A little of thy steadfastness,
Rounded with leafy gracefulness,
   Old oak, give me, —
That the world's blasts may round me blow,
And I yield gently to and fro,
While my stout-hearted trunk below   10
   And firm-set roots unshaken be.

Some of thy stern, unyielding might,
Enduring still through day and night
Rude tempest-shock and withering blight, —
   That I may keep at bay
The changeful April sky of chance
And the strong tide of circumstance, —
   Give me, old granite gray.

Some of thy pensiveness serene,
Some of thy never-dying green,   30
  Put in this scrip of mine, —
That griefs may fall like snow-flakes light,
And deck me in a robe of white,
Ready to be an angel bright, —
    O sweetly mournful pine.

A little of thy merriment,
Of thy sparkling, light content,
  Give me, my cheerful brook, —
That I may still be full of glee
And gladsomeness, where'er I be,   30
Though fickle fate hath prisoned me
    In some neglected nook.

Ye have been very kind and good
To me, since I've been in the wood,
  Ye have gone nigh to fill my heart;
But good-bye, kind friends, every one,
I've far to go ere set of sun;
  Of all good things I would have part,
  The day was high ere I could start,
And so my journey's scarce begun.   40

Heaven help me! how could I forget
To beg of thee, dear violet!
   Some of thy modesty,
That flowers here as well, unseen,
As if before the world thou'dst been,
O give, to strengthen me.

BEAVER BROOK

Hushed with broad sunlight lies the hill,
  And minuting the long day's loss,
The cedar's shadow,° slow and still,
  Creeps o'er its dial of gray moss.

Warm noon brims full the valley's cup,
  The aspen's° leaves are scarce astir,
Only the little mill sends up
  Its busy, never-ceasing burr.

Climbing the loose-piled wall that hems
  The road along the mill-pond's brink,
From 'neath the arching barberry-stems,
  My footstep scares the shy chewink.°

Beneath a bony buttonwood
  The mill's red door lets forth the din;
The whitened miller, dust-imbued,
  Flits past the square of dark within.

No mountain torrent's strength is here;
   Sweet Beaver, child of forest still,
Heaps its small pitcher° to the ear,
   And gently waits the miller's will.   20

Swift slips Undine° along the race
   Unheard, and then, with flashing bound,
Floods the dull wheel with light and grace,
   And laughing, hunts the loath drudge round.

The miller dreams not at what cost
   The quivering millstones hum and whirl,
Nor how, for every turn are tost
   Armfuls of diamond and of pearl.

But Summer cleared my happier eyes
   With drops of some celestial juice,   30
To see how Beauty underlies
   Forevermore each form of Use.

And more: methought I saw that flood,
   Which now so dull and darkling steals,
Thick, here and there, with human blood,
   To turn the world's laborious wheels.

No more than doth the miller there,
  Shut in our several cells, do we
Know with what waste of beauty rare
  Moves every day's machinery.   40

Surely the wiser time shall come
  When this fine overplus of might,
No longer sullen, slow and dumb,
  Shall leap to music and to light.

In that new childhood of the Earth
  Life of itself shall dance and play,
Fresh blood through Time's shrunk veins
      make mirth,
  And labor meet delight half-way.

MY LOVE°

Not as all other women are
  Is she that to my soul is dear;
Her glorious fancies come from far,
Beneath the silver evening-star,
  And yet her heart is ever near.

Great feelings hath she of her own,
  Which lesser souls may never know;
God giveth them to her alone,
And sweet they are as any tone
  Wherewith the wind may choose to blow.   10

Yet in herself she dwelleth not,
  Although no home were half so fair;
No simplest duty is forgot,
Life hath no dim and lowly spot
  That doth not in her sunshine share.

She doeth little kindnesses,
  Which most leave undone, or despise;

F

For naught that sets one heart at ease,
And giveth happiness or peace,
  Is low-esteemèd in her eyes.   20

She hath no scorn of common things,
  And, though she seem of other birth,
Round us her heart entwines and clings,
And patiently she folds her wings
  To tread the humble paths of earth.

Blessing she is: God made her so,
  And deeds of weekday holiness
Fall from her noiseless as the snow,
Nor hath she ever chanced to know
  That aught were easier than to bless.   30

She is most fair, and thereunto
  Her life doth rightly harmonize;
Feeling or thought that was not true
Ne'er made less beautiful the blue
  Unclouded heaven of her eyes.

She is a woman: one in whom
  The spring-time of her childish years
Hath never lost its fresh perfume,

Though knowing well that life hath room
  For many blights and many tears.   40

I love her with a love as still
  As a broad river's peaceful might,
Which, by high tower and lowly mill,
Goes wandering at its own will,
  And yet doth ever flow aright.

And, on its full, deep breast serene,
  Like quiet isles my duties lie;
It flows around them and between,
And makes them fresh and fair and green,
  Sweet homes wherein to live and die.   5c

THE BIRCH TREE°

Rippling through thy branches goes the sunshine,
  Among thy leaves that palpitate for ever;
Ovid in thee a pining Nymph had prisoned,
  The soul once of some tremulous inland river,
Quivering to tell her woe, but, ah! dumb, dumb for
    ever!

While all the forest, witched with slumberous moon-
      shine,
  Holds up its leaves in happy, happy silence,
Waiting the dew, with breath and pulse suspended, —
  I hear afar thy whispering, gleamy islands,
And track thee wakeful still amid the wide-hung
    silence.   10

Upon the brink of some wood-nestled lakelet,
  Thy foliage, like the tresses of a Dryad,
Dripping about thy slim white stem, whose shadow
  Slopes quivering down the water's dusky quiet,
Thou shrink'st as on her bath's edge would some
    startled Dryad.

Thou art the go-between of rustic lovers;
　Thy white bark has their secrets in its keeping;
Reuben writes here the happy name of Patience,
　And thy lithe boughs hang murmuring and weeping
Above her, as she steals the mystery from thy
　　keeping.　　　　　　　　　　　　　　　　20

Thou art to me like my beloved maiden,
　So frankly coy, so full of trembly confidences;
Thy shadow scarce seems shade, thy pattering leaflets
　Sprinkle their gathered sunshine o'er my senses,
And Nature gives me all her summer confidences.

Whether my heart with hope or sorrow tremble,
　Thou sympathizest still; wild and unquiet,
I fling me down; thy ripple, like a river,
　Flows valleyward, where calmness is, and by it
My heart is floated down into the land of quiet.　　30

THE SIRENS°

THE sea is lonely, the sea is dreary,
The sea is restless and uneasy;
Thou seekest quiet, thou art weary,
Wandering thou know'st not whither;
Our little isle is green and breezy,
Come and rest thee!   O come hither!
Come to this peaceful home of ours,
   Where evermore
The low west-wind creeps panting up the shore
To be at rest among the flowers;   10
Full of rest, the green moss lifts,
   As the dark waves of the sea
Draw in and out of rocky rifts,
   Calling solemnly to thee
With voices deep and hollow, —
    "To the shore
   Follow! O follow!
To be at rest forevermore!
  Forevermore!"

Look how the gray old Ocean   20
From depths of his heart rejoices,
Heaving with a gentle motion,
When he hears our restful voices;
List how he sings in an undertone,
Chiming with our melody;
And all sweet sounds of earth and air
Melt into one low voice alone,
That murmurs over the weary sea, —
And seems to sing from everywhere, —
  "Here may'st thou harbor peacefully,   30
Here may'st thou rest from the aching oar;
  Turn thy curvèd prow ashore,
And in our green isle rest forevermore!
  Forevermore!"
    And Echo half wakes in the wooded hill,
    And, to her heart so calm and deep,
    Murmurs over in her sleep,
Doubtfully pausing and murmuring still,
  "Evermore!"
      Thus on Life's weary sea,   40
      Heareth the marinere
      Voices sweet, from far and near,
      Ever singing low and clear,
      Ever singing longingly.

Is it not better here to be,
Than to be toiling late and soon?
In the dreary night to see
Nothing but the blood-red moon
Go up and down into the sea;
Or, in the loneliness of day,   50
    To see the still seals only
Solemnly lift their faces gray,
    Making it yet more lonely?
    Is it not better, than to hear
Only the sliding of the wave
Beneath the plank and feel so near
A cold and lonely grave,
A restless grave, where thou shalt lie
Even in death unquietly?
Look down beneath thy wave-worn bark,   60
    Look over the side and see
The leaden eye of the side-long shark
    Upturnèd patiently,
    Ever waiting there for thee:
Look down and see those shapeless forms,
    Which ever keep their dreamless sleep
    Far down within the gloomy deep,
And only stir themselves in storms,
Rising like islands from beneath,

And snorting through the angry spray,   70
As the frail vessel perisheth
In the whirls of their unwieldy play;
    Look down!   Look down!
Upon the seaweed, slimy and dark,
That waves its arms so lank and brown,
    Beckoning for thee!
Look down beneath thy wave-worn bark
    Into the cold depth of the sea!
    Look down!   Look down!
      Thus, on Life's lonely sea,   80
      Heareth the marinere
      Voices sad from far and near,
      Ever singing full of fear,
      Ever singing drearfully.

Here all is pleasant as a dream;
The wind scarce shaketh down the dew,
The green grass floweth like a stream
    Into the ocean's blue;
    Listen! O listen!
Here is a gush of many streams,   90
    A song of many birds,
And every wish and longing seems
Lulled to a numbered flow of words, —

Listen!   O listen!
Here ever hum the golden bees
Underneath full-blossomed trees,
At once with glowing fruit and flowers crowned; —
The sand is so smooth, the yellow sand,
That thy keel will not grate as it touches the land;
All around, with a slumberous sound   100
The singing waves slide up the strand,
And there, where the smooth, wet pebbles be,
　The waters gurgle longingly,
As if they fain would seek the shore,
To be at rest from the ceaseless roar,
To be at rest forevermore, —
　Forevermore!
　　Thus, on Life's gloomy sea,
　　Heareth the marinere
　　Voices sweet, from far and near,   110
　　Ever singing in his ear,
　　"Here is rest and peace for thee!"

NANTASKET, July, 1840.

THE COURTIN'

ZEKLE crep' up, quite unbeknown,
  An' peeked in thru' the winder,
An' there sot Huldy all alone,
  'Ith no one nigh to hender.

Agin the chimbly crooknecks° hung,
  An' in amongst 'em rusted
The ole queen's arm thet gran'ther Young
  Fetched back from Concord busted.

The wannut logs shot sparkles out
  Towards the pootiest, bless her!   10
An' leetle fires danced all about
  The chiny on the dresser.

The very room, coz she wuz in,
  Looked warm frum floor to ceilin',
And she looked full ez rosy agin
  Ez th' apples she wuz peelin'.

She heerd a foot an' knowed it, tu,
   A raspin' on the scraper, —
All ways to once her feelins flew
   Like sparks in burnt-up paper.   20

He kind of l'itered on the mat,
   Some doubtfle o' the seekle;
His heart kep' goin' pity-pat,
   But hern went pity Zekle.

An' yet she gin her cheer a jerk
   Ez though she wished him furder,
An' on her apples kep' to work
   Ez ef a wager spurred her.°

"You want to see my Pa, I spose?"
   "Wal, no; I come designin' — "   30
"To see my Ma?   She's sprinklin' cloe's
   Agin to-morrow's i'nin'."

He stood a spell on one foot fust
   Then stood a spell on tother,
An' on which one he felt the wust
   He couldn't ha' told ye, nuther.

Sez he, "I'd better call ag'in,"
   Sez she, "Think likely, Mister;"
The last word pricked him like a pin,
   An'—wal, he up an' kist her.   40

When Ma bimeby upon 'em slips,
   Huldy sot pale ez ashes,
All kind o' smily round the lips,
   An' teary round the lashes.

Her blood riz quick, though, like the tide
   Down to the Bay of Fundy.
An' all I know is they wuz cried
   In meetin', come nex Sunday.

THE CHANGELING°

I HAD a little daughter,
    And she was given to me
To lead me gently backward
    To the Heavenly Father's knee,
That I, by the force of nature,
    Might in some dim wise divine
The depth of his infinite patience
    To this wayward soul of mine.

I know not how others saw her,
    But to me she was wholly fair,   10
And the light of the heaven she came from
    Still lingered and gleamed in her hair;
For it was as wavy and golden,
    And as many changes took,
As the shadows of sun-gilt ripples
    On the yellow bed of a brook.

To what can I liken her smiling
    Upon me, her kneeling lover,

How it leaped from her lips to her eyelids,
 And dimpled her wholly over, 20
Till her outstretched hands smiled also,
 And I almost seemed to see
The very heart of her mother
 Sending sun through her veins to me!

She had been with us scarce a twelvemonth,
 And it hardly seemed a day,
When a troop of wandering angels
 Stole my little daughter away;
Or perhaps those heavenly Zingari°
 But loosed the hampering strings, 30
And when they had opened the cage-door,
 My little bird used her wings.

But they left in her stead a changeling,
 A little angel child,
That seems like her bud in full blossom,
 And smiles as she never smiled:
When I wake in the morning I see it
 Where she always used to lie,
And I feel as weak as a violet°
 Alone 'neath the awful sky. 40

As weak, yet as trustful also;
    For the whole year long I see
All the wonders of faithful Nature
    Still worked for the love of me;
Winds wander and dews drip earthward,
    Rains fall, suns rise and set,
Earth whirls, and all but to prosper
    A poor little violet.

This child is not mine as the first was,
    I cannot sing it to rest,
I cannot lift it up fatherly
    And bliss° it upon my breast;
Yet it lies in my little one's cradle,
    And it sits in my little one's chair,
And the light of the heaven she's gone to
    Transfigures its golden hair.

50

NOTES

THE VISION OF SIR LAUNFAL

The Metre. Except for the first eight lines, the poem is in mixed tetrameter, that is, in lines of four accents, separated by either one or two light syllables. Take, for example, the lines : —

> " Not only around our infancy
> Doth heaven with all its splendors lie."

In each of these we find four stressed or accented syllables :

> Not ónly aróund our ínfancý
> Doth héaven with áll its spléndors líe.

If we divide these lines into groups, — just as we divide music into bars, — and call these groups *feet*, we shall find that, as one reads the lines aloud, he will naturally hurry the time in groups where there are three syllables, so as to make them take only as long as the feet that have two. That is, no matter how many syllables there are in the foot, the time between accents is the same, the loud syllables coming with the regular beat of a drum. Beat time as you read the verses and you will see this.

In some verse there is a set number of syllables to each foot. Sometimes the feet are regularly of two syllables each, and, if they begin with the light syllable, are called *iambic*. In other forms all the feet are of three syllables, the line beginning with two light syllables. Such lines are called *anapestic*. In this poem the two forms are, as we have seen, combined, with a varied, irregular effect. Perhaps Lowell had in mind the irregular metre of Coleridge's *Christabel*, one of the first poems written in this free style. Some lines, it will be noted, begin with the accented syllable, no light syllable preceding. In short, the chief requirement in this form of verse is merely that there be four accented syllables to the line, more than two syllables seldom intervening between the accents.

There are few lines of three feet, usually at the end of a division of the poem, such as lines 79, 99, 154, and some others that the student can find for himself. One line, 123, has only two feet, and lines 227 and 228 are really parts of a single line printed as two. All these variations are intended to produce certain effects upon the ear. Observe what these effects are and how they are appropriate.

The first eight lines are in five feet, most of them beginning with a light syllable. From the number of feet this metre is called pentameter ; from the light beginning it is called iambic. Two lines, the first and fifth, do not begin with a light syllable. In this case, however, there are as many syllables as if they did, like the rest. The difference is that the accent has been made to fall ahead of time, where the light syllable ought by rights to be, just as might happen in syncopation in music.

Be sure, in reading the poem aloud, to bring out the music of the verse. Do not, of course, read it in "sing-song," which takes no account of the writer's meaning, but do not read it as if it were prose. Place the accented syllables regularly, almost as you would do in music, but bring out the full meaning at the same time. You may occasionally vary, retard, hasten, even contradict the rhythmical accent, but the rhythm and the rhyme must always be felt as underlying, — or the verse ceases to be verse. The true poet loves the sound of his verse no less than the thought, — if, indeed, he is able to think of the two as separable: to him they are rather one and indivisible. One should enter his magic land reverently.

PRELUDE TO PART FIRST

The two long Preludes introduce each part. But they do more than that. If they did not, their length, compared with that of what they introduce, would be indefensible. Besides preparing for the story, they give the spirit of it, the mood that it is to exemplify, the lesson that it is to illustrate. It is like a lecture with dissolving views. The poet shows us a landscape embodying the emotional spirit of his story before setting before us the story itself. We get first the mood, then the events with which it is to be associated. The first Prelude gives us the joy of summer, the inspiration that lies in the world of nature about us, a world that is full of reminders of our higher selves. It is full of the rapture of the season when goodness *seems* easy, when resolves blossom unforced. It wanders from thought to thought, perhaps bewilderingly, but always nearing its central theme.

ll. 1–8. The introductory stanza, the prelude to the prelude, gives some hint of this spirit. The poet, like the organist, who sits idly at the keys, and "knows not what he is playing," is to ponder as he will till his subject dawns clearly before him. He must bridge over the gulf between the dreamland of his story and the everyday present. The prelude aims to take up the reader in his ordinary mood and lead him, bit by bit, into the mood of the vision. In spite of this excuse, however, it should be noted that the poet strays too far from his central theme. The poem lacks clear structure and singleness of purpose. Much that is in itself delightful is quite irrelevant to his main object.

l. 6. **theme** is his subject, the musical idea that forms the basis of a musical composition. Most common "tunes" are all theme. In more complex work the theme is developed, expanded, and varied till a whole musical structure is reared upon it.

l. 8. **Auroral.** Like the flushes of dawn foretelling the coming of the sun.

l. 8. **Wavering vistas.** These glimmers of the dawning subject brighten along the cloud-passages of his vision, passages wavering and fluctuating.

ll. 9–32. In these lines there is a distinct answer to Wordsworth's *Ode on Intimations of Immortality*. It is not a denial so much as it is an amendment, a point of view subtly different. Wordsworth tells us : —

> "Heaven lies about us in our infancy!
>   Shades of the prison-house begin to close
>   Upon the growing boy,

> But he beholds the light, and whence it flows,
> He sees it in his joy;
> The youth, who daily further from the east
> Must travel, still is Nature's priest,
> And by the vision splendid
> Is on his way attended;
> At length the man perceives it die away
> And fade into the light of common day."

That it does *seem* to fade, Lowell admits, but he denies that this must be, for its apparent fading is owing merely to our blindness. The glory is still there, could we see it. Nature lies about us, full of inspiration for those whose eyes are open; and through sea, mountain, and forest she struggles to rouse the best in us.

l. 12. **Sinais.** Heights where we might, if we would, meet God face to face. But our souls are too little to be concerned about him. We "cringe," rather, and "plot," like Kipling's "little men of little soul," who "awoke to buy and sell again," unconscious of the daily miracles about them.

l. 14. Why **fallen** and **traitor**? Traitor to what? Fallen from what?

l. 15. In what sense do the winds utter prophecies? What may a prophecy do besides predicting? Did all the prophets of the Old Testament predict?

l. 16. **The mountain strives.** How? Why does it suggest strength?

l. 17. **Druid wood.** The Druids held forests sacred; the word seems also to imply comparison between the hoary trees and their aged priests. Think of the opening lines of *Evangeline*. The arms of the trees are outstretched in benediction, "*benedicite*" being the imperative of the Latin word meaning *bless*.

l. 20. **Shouts.** By the dash of its breakers and the roar of the surf.

l. 21. **Earth gets its price.** In apparent denial of the statement of Wordsworth : —

> " Earth fills her lap with pleasures of her own. . . .
>   The homely nurse doth all she can
> To make her foster-child, her inmate man
>   Forget the glories he hath known,
>   And that imperial palace whence he came."

But does not Lowell's " Earth " mean something different from Wordsworth's ? Lowell seems to be speaking of the world of men, Wordsworth of the world of nature. Wordsworth's " Earth " seems to have had some element of Lowell's " Heaven."

l. 23. **Shrives.** Receives confession and gives absolution.

l. 25. **At the devil's booth.** Even the pleasures of sin have their price.

l. 27. **A cap and bells.** The marks of the court fool. We trade our lives for some trifle of fame, some mere bubble. worth nothing after all.

l. 30. **'Tis only God.** Realize the force of the contrast between the good of Earth and the good of Heaven. For one " Earth gets its price " ; the other is " given for the asking." This seems to have been a favorite idea of Lowell's. In a letter written when he was but twenty-one, we find him saying that at whatever price other things are sold and bartered, —

> " Nature is ever had, free gratis,
> 'Children half-price,' as 'twas of old."

Observe the transition, in line 32, to the next subject. The poet passes on to the idea of June, as the organist, letting his fingers wander as they list, passes from theme to theme till he finds the right one.

l. 33. **June.** June seems to have been Lowell's favorite month. His letters are full of raptures over it, and in *Under the Willows* we find him representing the bobolink as singing in his ecstacy : —

> "June ! Dear June ! Now God be praised for June !"

Lines 33 to 56 might well be memorized. This is the best passage in literature descriptive of our American summer. Its one fault is that it is not directly helpful to the main purpose of the poem.

Readers not in New England should note that it is the New England June that is described. In other parts of the country, the season that Lowell has in mind appears earlier. But in that part of New England north of Cape Cod the summer comes slowly. "May," as Lowell put it, "is often more like Mayn't," and one must wait till the time when "our Spring gits everythin' in tune."

l. 35. What musical instrument has Lowell in mind ? What is the picture ?

l. 38. **Murmur** in what? **Glisten** in what?

l. 42. **Climbs to a soul.** The grass and flowers seem to be the soul of the earth, made visible in green life. Note the idea of groping toward the light.

l. 43. **"The flush of life."** Swinburne has:—

> "The faint fresh flame of the young year flushes
> From leaf to flower and flower to fruit."

It is as if a green flame were kindling and catching everywhere.

l. 45. The **cowslip** of New England is not the cowslip of England, but the marsh-marigold. It grows in marshy meadows, and has a bright flower, not unlike that of the buttercup.

Startles: starts up. Or it may mean, startles the eye with its flash of gold.

l. 46. **Chalice,** of course, means cup. Is there anything appropriate in the fact that it usually denotes a golden, precious, even a sacred vessel?

l. 48. **Some happy creature's.** What kind of creature?

l. 49. **At his door.** At the door of what?

l. 50. Why **atilt**? Why like a **blossom**? What kind of bird had Lowell in mind?—Is it the bobolink?

l. 51. How does this deluge break out? Have you ever seen a bird that seemed to be trying to express the joy of the whole springtime?

l. 54. What, in the metre of this line, makes it a trifle harsh? See also line 49. 53-57. What is her "song"? In what may hers be the equal of his? What *is* the better?

l. 56. **The nice ear.** What does "nice" mean here? See the dictionary. Which meaning fits?

l. 57. **The high-tide.** What is the low-tide of the year, when life seems to have ebbed away? This figure would be especially vivid to Lowell, who, from his windows, could look out in the broad salt-marshes of the Charles and see the inlets and creeks sucked empty and brown at low water, or flooded to the green grass-tops with the great fulness of the new-moon tide. In another poem Lowell speaks of "all life washed clear in the high-tide of the year."

l. 67. Note the effective indirect description in line 67 and the lines following.

l. 71. What is **maize**? What is meant by saying that it has sprouted?

l. 72. Note how this line brings out the blue of both sky and river. See *Indian Summer Reverie*, p. 18.

l. 73. Our American robin, the migratory or red-breasted thrush, not the robin redbreast of England. But, whatever his name, Lowell liked him, and watched his ways. In the *Biglow Papers*, he says:—

> "Thets robin-redbreast's almanick; he knows
> Thet arter this ther's only blossom-snows;
> So, choosin' out a handy crotch an' spouse,
> He goes to plastrin' his adobè house."

With regard to this whole description, it must be noted that spring is a prominent force in all Lowell's letters and in poems. It seems to be the season that he felt most intensely. One finds him dwelling on it in scraps of description throughout his letters. He longs to leave his "lectures and articles," and to be out enjoying it all. It shows him, he says, "what a poet God is." For the whole springtime is God's poem, sung over and over, yet always new. And he declares that he has only now discovered the meaning of the buttercup "in the third stanza" of this divine lay. But he will keep the solution to himself.

l. 77. **Bold chanticleer** was another favorite of Lowell's. Again and again we find him referred to, usually in words not unlike those in the poem. He writes to friends that everything is safe at their house or else their chanticleer lied, "for he crowed with a lusty satisfaction."

l. 78. What is the "new wine of the year"? Compare this figure with that in lines 50–51.

l. 79. Note this line is shorter than the rest, having only three feet instead of four.

ll. 83–85. Goodness is as easy as happiness, or seems as easy. Does the First Part seem to show that it is? Is not this feeling often deceptive, or even a sign of pride and selfishness?

ll. 86–87. What is compared to the clouds that leave no track in the unscarred heaven? What resemblance?

ll. 90–93. What new figure begins in line 90? To what is the new peace of the heart compared? In what lies the resemblance?

l. 91. What are the "rifts"? What picture intended?

l. 93. Why **healed**? In what sense can snow "heal" a crater?

l. 94. Note that the organist has at last reached his theme. The subject has taken shape and the story is to begin. There is no sharp break between the Prelude and the poem itself. The first leads smoothly into the second, with a sudden yet smoothly effected change to the unexpected, giving an impression of dream. Sir Launfal appears as mysteriously yet as fittingly as the ship in the *Ancient Mariner.*

PART FIRST

In prose there would be explanation as to who Sir Launfal was. In a poem so lyric, that is, so emotional and imaginative as this, explanation would interfere with the simple expression of feeling. To stop to explain is to drop into prose, to relapse into the commonplace. Poetry has less patience than prose. One must merely hint the explanation between the lines, and the reader, for the sake of the intensity of the feeling conveyed to him, must be willing to make the added effort necessary to grasp the facts of the story. The poem cannot be skimmed, like an exciting tale in prose, but must be read slowly, with attention to the pictures hinted in every word.

Do not trouble yourself with the historical basis of the story. Lowell, as you may see by the note on p. 93, did have in mind a definite legend. His setting for his story, however, avoids the limitation of any particular place or period. Sir Launfal is the knight of feudal days — probably in or near the period of the crusades. But we no more ask in what year or what county of the "north countree" he lived than we ask in what year or from what port the Ancient Mariner's vessel set sail on her mysterious voyage. The story is true to human life and natural beauty as a whole, — not in any one momentary manifestation.

It will be well for the reader to have a good idea of the world of chivalry, of knights, armor, castles, and of the great religious "quests" of tradition and history. Read Tennyson's *Idylls of the King*, Lanier's *The Boy's King Arthur*, Scott's *Ivanhoe, Talisman, Abbot,* and *Monastery,* and see if these old-world realities do not assume reality in your mind. Put yourself, in short — so far as in your power lies — in the days described, and in the spirit of the poet. This only of the artificial elements. The out-of-door scenes are the familiar scenes of New England. One needs only to open one's eyes to them.

In explanation of the quest on which the young knight is to set forth, Lowell says: "According to the mythology of the Romancers, the San Greal, or Holy Grail, was the cup out of which Jesus partook of the last supper with his disciples. It was brought into England by Joseph of Arimathea, and remained there, an object of pilgrimage and adoration, for many years in the keeping of his lineal descendants. It was incumbent upon those who had charge of it to be chaste in thought, word, and deed; but one of the keepers having broken this condition, the Holy Grail disappeared. From that time it was a favorite enterprise of the knights of Arthur's court to go in search of it. Sir Galahad was at last successful in finding it, as may be read in the seventeenth book of the *Romance of King*

Arthur. Tennyson has made Sir Galahad the subject of one of the most exquisite of his poems.

"The plot (if I may give that name to anything so slight) of the following poem is my own, and, to serve its purposes, I have enlarged the circle of competition in search of the miraculous cup in such a manner as to include, not only other persons than the heroes of the Round Table, but also a period of time subsequent to the date of King Arthur's reign."

While the story of Sir Launfal seems to have been entirely of Lowell's devising, we do find, in early romances, references to a knight of a similar name, and it was probably the reading of these that suggested to the poet the name of his hero.

Sir Launfal, or rather "Lanval," is the hero of a poem written by Thomas Chestre (who lived in the reign of Henry VI.) and to be found in Ritson's *English Metrical Romances.* The story has, in a very few points, a slight resemblance to Lowell's. Sir Lanval

> "gaf gyftys largelyche
> Gold and sylver; and clodes ryche,
> To squyer and to knycht."

On account of his bounty he is made King Arthur's steward. He afterward, like Sir Launfal in his vision, becomes poor, but is supplied by a lady-love — not by the simple process of awaking from a bad dream — with gold and riches.

l. 97. What shows the knight's lack of humility?

l. 100. **Never a bed.** It is not uncommon in old romances, to read of knights watching their armor or sleeping by it on the night before setting out on a quest. The young knight has,

too, the hope that some vision will be granted to him.   As was
shown in the Introduction (p. ix), the young Lowell was not
a little of a dreamer and visionary himself.

l. 103.   **Rushes** were the ordinary covering for the floor
of a castle in mediæval days.

l. 105.   With each day the world, for each of us, is recreated.
Out of the blank, dark, and apparent annihilation of the night,
each sight comes back as if made anew.   Shakespeare speaks
of sleep as the "death of each day's life."

l. 107.   Why like a **cloud**?   What is the resemblance?
How does the figure help?   *floated*

l. 108.   Why into his **soul**?   Why not his mind?   Of what
nature was the vision?   *like a dream*

l. 108.   What follows is a dream.   Sir Launfal does not
actually leave his bed on the rushes till he awakes "as from a
swound," in line 328.   All between, — the leaving the castle,
the sight of the leper to whom he throws the coin, the suffering
from cold and want, the apparition of the Christ, — all these
are but appearances in his dream, — the Divine Revelation in
the hope of which he fell asleep.

l. 109.   The picture that follows is seen in his dream.   It
doubles the impression of the summer picture in the prelude,
but does not repeat any definite features of it.

l. 109.   Why **flapped over**?   Why not *flew over*?

l. 114.   Summer is represented as besieging the castle.
Note that throughout the poem summer is made symbolic of

kindliness, charity, warm human feeling, while the winter seems to symbolize reserve and heartlessness. The cold castle shuts out all the summer's attempts to bring in a warmer, kinder feeling. Just as its chill gray stone refuses to respond to the green flame of the season, so its spirit is inaccessible to any kindly warmth.

l. 115. Winter has retreated. This castle alone represents it in the land of the enemy.

l. 116. **In the North Countree.** In the north of England. The scenery, however, is rather that of New England. The form "Countree" is adopted here partly for quaint effect, partly for rhyme.

l. 118. This selfishness reacts, later in his vision, on Sir Launfal himself. The seneschal "shouts the wanderer away from the porch."

l. 121. **Scale.** Climb up and over.

l. 125. The **tents** are the trees. It is a pretty picture. See how each descriptive touch applies to them.

l. 127. **Fell off.** Why not *died out?* What difference of suggestion?

l. 128. **Surly clang** and **dark arch** give the tone of the castle.

l. 129. What kind of horse was a "charger"? *a large dash*

l. 130. **The maiden knight.** A young knight as unversed in war as a maiden is in the mature life of woman.

l. 131. How would he look? Imagine the picture.

l. 135. Why a **sheaf**? Why "all" the **rays**? Why had the sun shot the rays over the wall of the castle ? To what are they compared ?

l. 136. The young knight is in accord with the surly castle only in hardness of heart. In all else he is in accord with the brightness of the summer.

l. 137. Why as a **locust-leaf**? Is it lighter than other leaves ? Recall its appearance. Why is it easier to imagine a particular leaf than any leaf.

l. 138. **Unscarred** because he was a "maiden knight," with all his conflicts before him.

l. 146. **The pitcher-plant's cup.** See dictionary or botany for an illustration. Why into a picture of castles and knights, does Lowell introduce a plant peculiar to America ? Does it impair the effect ? What is the result upon those not familiar with the plant mentioned ? In what sense, by the way, did the season "brim" all things up ? What previous comparison was a little like this ? See lines 57–61.

l. 147. **Made morn.** Came into full day, perhaps somewhat as a vessel may be said to "make port," to "make the coast." Or it may mean that his bright armor *made morning* through the darkness of the arch. The first meaning seems the better here, since we are to see the picture, in this sentence, through Sir Launfal's eyes.

l. 148. **A leper.** Leprosy is among the most repulsive of diseases. In the Middle Ages it was fairly common in Europe. There are many references to it in the Old Testament.

l. 149. **Who begged with his hand.** How does this detail

aid the picture ? Note how far it affects the scene that you
see in your mind.

ll. 150–154. Are these figures of value ? What purpose does
each serve. See why each is true, why each brings out the intensity of the young knight's loathing.

l. 155. Not "foul of stature." The phrase modifies only
the second adjective. Is "of stature" logically necessary to
the meaning ?

l. 156. **His dainty nature.** Is there not a touch of scorn in
the words ? Do not lines 96 and 97 perhaps justify it ?

l. 158. **So he tossed him a piece of gold in scorn.** This is
the central action of the poem, the wrong deed upon which, as
upon the killing of the Albatross in the *Ancient Mariner*, the
whole plot turns. Observe that the wrongdoing is not in the
gift of gold, but in the feeling that this frees the giver from any
claim of sympathy. Sir Launfal wants to evade his responsi-
bilities as a fellow human being, to "compound his obligations"
for money.

l. 160. **The poor man's crust.** Compare line 295.

l. 161. Be careful to understand the inverted order. "That
which the hand can hold is no true alms." The word alms,
though ending with "s," is singular. Be sure you get the
spirit of the beggar's words : It is not the gift itself that is
of worth but the spirit of love that goes with it.

l. 166. **A slender mite.** A reference to the New Testament.
The passage has a significant resemblance to this. It may even
have suggested to Lowell the moral of his poem : —

H

" And Jesus sat over against the treasury, and beheld how the people cast money into the treasury : and many that were rich cast in much. And there came a poor widow, and she cast in two mites, which make a farthing. And he called unto him his disciples, and said unto them, Verily I say unto you, This poor widow cast in more than all they which are casting into the treasury : for they all did cast in of their superfluity ; but she of her want did cast in all that she had, even all her living." — Mark xii. 42.

l. 168. **That thread of the all-sustaining Beauty,** that runs through all. Lowell seemed to feel with particular intensity this presence of pervading soul. In one of his letters (see p. ix), he tells how, at one moment, and, while he would not write what he felt, he saw the central secret of all systems. " God," he said, " is the secret, the spring, source and centre of all Beauty."

l. 170. **His alms.** The alms given by him who gives to the God in man.

ll. 170–171. True alms is given not to the hand but to the heart. Compare line 163.

l. 172. **A god goes with it.** Why not " God " ? What does this mean ? In what sense is it true ? **Store** means abundance, plenty.

PRELUDE TO PART SECOND

The prelude of the second part gives us a picture of winter. The setting of the part itself is wintry. There is a double purpose in this. It emphasizes, first, the contrast between the youth and exuberance of Sir Launfal in his pride and the

humility of his later mood. And, through this, it shows us
that the season when it seems easy for the heart to be true is
not so likely to lead it to truth as the season of suffering and
humiliation. Besides this, there is a secondary signification :
the winter accords with the age of Sir Launfal. Its veins, like
his, are sapless and old. For further carrying out of this part
of the suggestion, see note on p. 105.

l. 174. The first line is ambiguous in scansion. It might, if
it stood in a different context, be read : —

Down swépt the chíll wind fróm the moúntain peák.

It must, however, to accord with the lines that follow, be
read : —

Down swépt the chill wínd from the moúntain peák.

It is, as a rule, important that the first line of a new part
should show the metre without possibility of mistake.

l. 174. **The mountain peak.** Are there such mountain peaks
in England ? Was Lowell necessarily placing the peak any-
where near the scene of his story ? Does he not speak of it
rather as the remote storehouse of the winter's cold ?

l. 175. The counting by **summers** implies the unmelting,
eternal snow.

l. 176. **Wold** as used here means open moorland, rolling,
barren land, where the wind has full sweep.

l. 178. The wind is so keen that it stings the face like
sleet.

l. 179. The feeling of dead, numb, pervading chill that precedes a snowstorm. See Whittier's *Snowbound* for another description and another set of vivid winter pictures.

l. 180. **Unleafed,** not "leafless" merely, but "despoiled of leaves."

l. 181. **The little brook** has a certain analogy to Sir Launfal. Under its wintry exterior, its life is still active, and it keeps the recollection and semblance of summer. Just so in his aged body (aged only in his vision, of course), his heart is still warm with human tenderness, — warmer, in fact, than in his summer of youth.

In December, 1848, the year when this poem was written, Lowell writes to his friend, C. F. Briggs, and describes a walk to Watertown; a walk taken the night before, over the snow, with the full moon before him. As he stood on the hill just above the village, the quiet of the night was broken only by the tinkle of a little brook that "ran too swiftly for frost to catch it." It was this brook, he says, that he had in mind in this description.

Compare also with the picture here lines 155–165, *An Indian Summer Reverie.*

l. 183. The stars on a frosty night seem unusually white and clear.

l. 184. A groin in architecture is the intersection of two arched vaults. See the illustration in an unabridged dictionary.

l. 185. **His crystal spars.** The slender ice-beams that he used as timbers.

l. 186. **As the lashes,** etc.   As the sharp rays of light that seem to flash out around a star.

l. 187.   Imagine these **halls** and **chambers.**   Fancy yourself small enough to enter them and walk, as Lowell invites you to, through the wonderland of the ice-roofed brook.

l. 189.   Observe how the word "tinkling" keeps the image vivid.

l. 190.   A **crypt** is an arched or vaulted passage.   A **forest-crypt** is a passage vaulted by overarching boughs of trees. Here the forest-crypt is "frost-leaved"; that is, its forest is wrought of ice.

l. 191. **Steel-stemmed.**   With stems cold and bright as steel.

l. 192.   As if a breeze bent them.

l. 193. **Fretwork.**   Interlaced ornamental work.   See illustration in dictionary.

l. 195. **In sharp relief.**   The design stood out boldly, in *alto relievo.*

l. 196. **Arabesques** are fanciful complicated designs, either of geometrical patterns or of animal and leaf forms.   Have you ever seen on the window panes in winter any pattern that could be described as **ice-fern leaf?**

l. 198. **The gladness of heaven.**   Not simply the daylight. What is the gain?

l. 201. **That crystalled.**   Each drop, in the light of sun or moon, was a miniature star.

l. 204.   A reference to the ice-built winter palace of the

Empress of Russia, Catherine II. Such palaces are sometimes erected at Canadian winter carnivals.

ll. 205–210. **Here the little brook is no longer the builder.** The roof is now a structure of the fairies, the frost-elves, who keep here the patterns of all the beauties of the summer, beauties that in summer the waters see reflected in their depths. What beauties of summer have been mentioned as "mimicked"? Can you think of others that might have been named? Lowell writes, in another poem, of streams that, like the brook here, keep a "summer mind," though "Snow-hid in Jenooary."

l. 211. **Within the hall.** Here the scene changes. We see the interior of Sir Launfal's castle. Some critic thinks that the mention of Christmas here is intended to lead to the mention of Christ in the part which this introduces. Do you think that Lowell had this intention? What does the warmth and cheer of Christmas emphasize? How does it help the main story? Note how it leads by contrast to the description of Sir Launfal's misery.

l. 212. **The cheeks of Christmas.** Of the Christmas feasters? or is Christmas personified?

l. 213. **A corbel** is a projecting support for a beam or cornice. See dictionary. It would afford — as it commonly does afford in churches — a good point from which to suspend festoons of evergreen. What figure in **sprouting**?

l. 214. **Lightsome.** Not light, but blithe, delightsome, cheery.

l. 215. **Through the deep gulf.** Lowell did not have to go to his imagination for a huge fireplace. An old colonial mansion like Elmwood abounded in them.   One finds in his letters many references.   He speaks of the northwest wind as "crowing lustily" in his chimney, and tells how he has "touched off" the heap of wood that, all summer long, has been waiting in the wide fireplace.

l. 216. **The Yule-log,** — a huge log burned at Christmas.   Its burning was a survival of an old heathen festival in honor of the god Thor.   The custom and the name of the feast — "Yuletide" — were continued into Christian times.

ll. 216–218. Watch, in fancy, the fire as you read.   Note the fitness of the descriptive words, — *wallows, droop, flap, belly, tug.*   To what comparison are all these appropriate ?   How does the comparison help the mental image ?

l. 220. **Hunted to death.**   What is hunting it to death ?   What are the **galleries** ?   Have you ever heard the sap **shrill** in this way ?

l. 223.   The idea of the soot-forest is fantastic, but is it too fantastic to suit the mood of one watching a roaring fire ?   What are the "tangled darks" ?   Try to imagine them.

l. 224.   Why **startled deer** ?   How would deer act if suddenly frightened by the approach of a stranger.

l. 227.   **And rattles and wrings.**   Is this figure true ?   Does it help ?   Why is it less effective than the other figures that we have noticed ?

l. 230.   Why a **Christmas carol** ?   What contrast is suggested by **of its own** ?   What possible irony ?

l. 231. The **burden** of a song is its refrain, or, sometimes, the prevailing idea.   Here it may be either — or both.

l. 233. **Seneschal.** The official who had charge of the household, the steward or majordomo.

l. 233. **Like a torch.** In what did his voice resemble one ? How does the comparison help ?   Who is the "wanderer" ?

l. 235. How does it come that the **gateway** is farther away than the **porch ?** What was the construction of a castle ?

l. 237. **Window-slits.** The windows or loop-holes of the castle were, on the outside, mere slits, — though on the inside they were wider.   See the illustration in the dictionary.

l. 238. What effect would the light shining through narrow slits produce upon the drifting snow without ?   Why against the **drift** of the cold ?   For what purpose are piers sometimes built out at angles to the shore ?

Observe how, at the end of this Part, as at the end of the first Prelude, the subject of Sir Launfal has been taken up.   Here, as there, he has entered the story unannounced, unexpected, yet, as is always the case in dreams, taking a place that seems his.   We never foresee the changes of our dreams, yet when they come we accept them as matters of course.   It seems, here, that rather too much is made of Sir Launfal.   The other Prelude merely mentioned him, and the Part that it introduced at once took up the story.   But here the Prelude *tells* some of the story, and the Second Part, beginning, as the Prelude does, with description, does not speak of him for some lines.   The

Prelude seems to steal some of the facts that should have been conveyed in the story itself. The plan is not carried out consistently with the first Prelude and Part I.

PART SECOND

The chill of the winter corresponds to the age of Sir Launfal as he sees himself in his dream.

l. 243. **For the weaver Winter.** In earlier editions this had read "for the frost's swift shuttles its shroud had spun." What improvement in the sound ? What loss in the vividness of the figure ?

l. 245. **Shed off.** How would shining feathers seem to shed off the light ? Think of the picture. Compare for general impression line 176, *An Indian Summer Reverie*.

l. 250. **Sir Launfal.** Remember that all this is in his dream. The real Sir Launfal, young as ever, lies asleep on the rushes.

l. 250. **Hard gate.** Who made the gate "hard" against the poor ? Is not this a case of what is called "poetic justice" ?

l. 251. What is an **earldom** ? See dictionary.

l. 255. He had, at setting out, worn a cross **blazoned** as a decoration on his **surcoat**, that is, the cloak worn over his armor. What has he learned since ?

l. 256. **The sign.** That is the cross.

l. 259. **Mail.** Does he wear mail now ? Why is the word used here ? What does the figure mean ?

l. 259. **Barbèd.** Pointed, toothed like a spear, — consequently, biting, keen. Scan the line and find the reason for giving the word two syllables.

ll. 264–272. What does this description show us with regard to Sir Launfal's travels ? How does it help the story by force of contrast ? What charm has it in itself ? Do these considerations justify the poet in inserting it here to interrupt the narrative ? Does it lead smoothly to the next point in the story ?

l. 264. **Snake-like.** How does this apply to a caravan ? Imagine the long line of camels.

l. 270. Be sure to see the appropriateness of the figure ? Imagine the spring, not a flowing spring, but a spring that comes bubbling fountain-like up out of the earth. In what would it be like an infant ? Why is the grass compared to a necklace ?

l. 272. Observe the change of figure in "waved its signal of palms." Is it not a long step from a little spring to a spring big enough to wave such a signal.

ll. 272–273. Why is the breaking off of the stanza with incomplete rhyme appropriate ? What corresponding interruption in Sir Launfal's thought ? Read the lines aloud and note the fitting of sound to sense.

l. 274. **Happy.** Why ? What particular reason for happiness lies before them ?

l. 278. **White.** See 2 Kings, v. 27. "And he went out

from his presence a leper as white as snow." What "ice-isles" are referred to ?

l. 281. **On the tree.**   On the cross.

l. 282. **Thy crown of thorns.**   Matt. xxvii. 29 ; Mark xv. 17.

l. 285.   John xx. 25, 27.

l. 287.   "Inasmuch as ye have done it unto one of the least of these my brethren, ye have done it unto me."   Matt. xxv. 40.

l. 288. **The soul . . . stood up.**   His soul, the inner spirit of man, shone through the imperfections of its bodily mantle.

l. 290. **Guise.**   See dictionary.

l. 291. **Leprosie.**   See note on *North Countree*, line 116.

l. 292. **When he girt.**   Changed from the earlier reading, "when he caged his young life." What improvement ? Is there any loss ?

l. 294. **Ashes and dust.**   Of what are these significant ? What is the signification of the name Ash Wednesday ? What biblical mention of "sackcloth and ashes" ?

ll. 300–301. **Yet with fine wheaten bread.**   It was the spirit of the gift, not the humble gift itself, that he perceived. The spirit transfigured it.   Observe the significance of "with his *soul.*"

l. 302. Why **mused** ?   Why was his face downcast ?   Of what was he thinking ?

l. 305.   Christ appears to him in his true form. He has passed the trial and learned the secret.

l. 307. **The Beautiful Gate.** "And a certain man lame from his mother's womb was . . . laid daily at the gate of the temple which is called Beautiful." Acts iii. 2.

l. 308. **Himself the Gate.** "I am the door; by me if any man enter in, he shall be saved." John x. 9. "I am the way, the truth, and the life : no man cometh unto the Father, but by me."

l. 310. What kind of **leaves** has the pine ? Note how quickly the figure changes.

l. 313. **The shaggy unrest.** Is the latter part of the comparison appropriate ? Was Sir Launfal's character full of unrest ? This line is hesitating in metre. One does not know whether to read, "*float* down upon," or "float *down* upon."

l. 314. **Calmer than silence.** What is not true literally is often true in suggestion. See what feeling is produced by the intentional contradiction. Is there not, perhaps, some reference to the " still, small voice " ? 1 Kings xix. 12.

l. 320. **This crust,** etc. Matt. xxvi. 26–28.
By this deed, by good works, done in the right spirit of love to all, Sir Launfal has entered into true communion with Christ. Notice, it is not what we give — not money coldly given to " get rid " of importunity — it is what we share, what we give as to a friend or brother, that benefits. How and in what sense does the giver feed Christ ? In what sense does he feed himself ?

l. 327. This is the end of the Vision. Sir Launfal awakes. He is still young, still rich and powerful. He has learned his lesson through adversity in dream, and may apply it to real life in prosperity.

l. 328. **A swound** is a swoon.   See *Ancient Mariner*, "Like noises in a *swound*."

l. 329. In what sense is the Grail found in his castle ? What has his lesson taught him ? What work is there for him to do at home ?

l. 332. **Stronger mail.**   Is there not, perhaps, a reference to Ephesians vi. 13–17. "Wherefore take unto you the whole armour of God. . . . Stand, therefore, having your loins girt about with truth, and having on the breastplate of righteousness . . . taking the shield of faith . . . and the helmet of salvation, and the sword of the Spirit, which is the word of God."

l. 336. **The hangbird.**   The oriole, a favorite of Lowell's. We find him writing, in his letters, of its nest near his window.

l. 338. **The Summer's long siege.**   A return of the figure from lines 119–127. Summer has won. She has captured Sir Launfal's heart as well as the castle. Every wanderer and outcast is welcome now.

Note how the return of this figure gives an impression of oneness or *unity* of plan.

l. 343. In what sense does summer **linger there the whole year round** ? Literally ?

l. 344. **A serf.**   See dictionary.

l. 345. **Bower.**   An inner or private room, as opposed to the more public **hall.** In what sense does the serf have " hall and bower at his command " ? See line 347 also.

l. 347. **Lord of the earldom.** In what sense? To what extent may this be taken literally ? Is it not a case of poetical exaggeration ? What is probably meant ? Would it be well if it were true literally ?

AN INDIAN SUMMER REVERIE

Indian Summer. The period of summer-like weather that comes in October or early November, accompanied usually by haze. The English call it " St. Martin's summer." The term " Indian Summer " is distinctly American.

l. 5. **Hebe Autumn.** Hebe was the cup-bearer of the gods. As she filled their golden bowl with wine, so autumn fills the valleys with haze.

l. 11. **My own projected spirit. . . .** It seems to be the writer's own mood, projected from his soul, that colors the whole world. " Steep " is a verb.

l. 25. **Ruth.** For story of her gleaning see Bible, Ruth, Chapter iii. The student will do well to become familiar with the whole story. In what sense does memory " glean "?

l. 32. **Magellan's Straits.** Where are they ? Why mentioned here ?

l. 35. **Quarry,** in what sense ? See dictionary ?

l. 50. **The birch.** Compare poem on p. 68. Why lady-like ?

l. 61. **Sees.** What is he to imagine ?

l. 80. **Whose** refers to " wall."

l. 91. **Martyr oak.** Why martyr ? What kind of martyr-dom is suggested ?

l. 104. A little like *Sir Launfal*, lines 31–32.

l. 147. **Simond's hill,** See description of Cambridge, Intro-duction, p. xii.

l. 156. **With smooth plate-armor.** Compare this with the description of " the fresh-sparred grots " and " little brook " in the Second Part of the *Vision of Sir Launfal.*

l. 160. What war, in 1847, would Lowell have in mind ?

l. 163. Waterfalls that the river creates, etc.

l. 176. The sunshine seems blown off by the bleak wind. See *Sir Launfal,* line 245.

l. 180. **Pearly breakers.** Compare the pictures in Whittier's *Snowbound.*

l. 190. **Druid-like, Stonehenge.** Stonehenge is noted for the huge blocks of stones that lie there or stand in strange combina-tions, — remains, it is thought, of some ancient Druid temple.

l. 209. **The Muses' factories.** The buildings of Harvard College, where the arts are " ground out."

l. 218. **The hillock's . . . house-bespotted swell,** etc. Low-ell probably refers to the houses south of Dana St. Apparently he does not altogether approve of their architecture !

l. 223. **Allston.** Washington Allston, the painter, 1799–1843, a noted figure in early Cambridge at the time of Lowell's boyhood. He painted merely historical paintings on biblical subjects. Some of his work may be found in the Boston Museum of Fine Arts. See Lowell's essay, *Cambridge Thirty Years Ago*.

l. 225. **Virgilium vidi tantum.** " I caught one glimpse of Virgil " (literally " I barely saw him "). A quotation often applied to such a glimpse of some celebrity. See Browning's poem, *Memorabilia*, for his impressions from such a meeting.

l. 227. **Undine-like.** Undine was a water nymph, graceful and fairy-like, described by Fouqué in a charming little romance (written in German). See *Beaver Brook*, line 21.

l. 228. **Down**, like thistledown, moving at the least breath of air.

l. 229. **Homestead.** Elmwood.

l. 234. **The village blacksmith.** See Longfellow's well-known poem.

l. 254. **The six old willows.** See Introduction, p. xvi. These trees afford the subject for a later poem, *Under the Willows*.

l. 255. **Paul Potter,** a famous Dutch painter of the seventeenth century.

l. 260. A stanza full of puns, of which Lowell was always fond. Horace says "it is a joy to have collected Olympic dust on one's chariot wheels." Lowell, making a punning use of the word *collegisse*, says that it is a joy to have "colleged." And he points out incidentally that the dust of Cambridge is to him dearer than that of Olympic origin.

The last two stanzas must be read thoughtfully. The student may find them hard to understand; the idea that they embody is one that may not have been brought to him. The poet has in mind the death of his little daughter. How much he felt this loss can be realized in part from reading his letters of that time. The volume in which this poem appeared is "reverently dedicated" "to the ever happy memory of our little Blanche." In the verses to his wife which open the volume, Lowell says : —

> "Death knits as well as parts, and still, I wis,
>   Her tender radiance shall enfold us here,
> Even as the light, borne up by inward bliss,
>   Threads the void glooms of space without a fear,
>   To print on farthest stars his pitying kiss."

See also *The Changeling*, p. 78, which speaks of the loss still more pathetically.

RHŒCUS

The central idea is that by evil, or merely by selfish deeds, one suffers in one's own character. Rhœcus loses, on account of his pettiness of nature, the power of seeing the vision that so enchanted him.

Lines 1–35 present an unnecessarily full discussion of the fact that in every human worship there is something uplifting, some noble lesson. Such apology is not needed. The poet would have done better had he let the story speak for itself.

l. 56. **Dryad.** The wood-nymph, whose life was bound up with the life of the tree which was her habitation.

l. 147. **Only the soul hath power o'er itself.** It is not she that is punishing him. His punishment is not inflicted from without, but is the direct result of his own deeds reacting on his own nature.

In earlier editions there followed some fifty lines of moralizing. The soul is, like Rhœcus, seeking ideal beauty, but is enticed by the world to forget its aspirations, and even to refuse heaven's warning messengers. Why is the poem better without this? Why are formal " morals " at the ends of stories seldom found in the work of great writers ?

THE BOBOLINK

This poem appeared in Lowell's first volume, *A Year's Life*, but for some reason was omitted in most of the succeeding collections. The omission was strange, as this poem would appear to most readers one of the best in the volume.

The Greek title is not easy to translate literally. **Gelasma** means *laughter*, while **Anerithmon** means *incalculable, beyond the reach of arithmetic.* Æschylus uses the phrase to convey the ripple and sparkle of the sea. The application to the bobolink is obvious.

l. 1. **Anacreon,** a noted Greek poet, who sung mainly of song, wine, flowers, and various delight.　In what is the bird like him ?

l. 14. **While thy loved-one.** With this description of the bird compare that in *An Indian Summer Reverie*, lines 127–133.

l. 40. **I seem again to be a boy.** This is really the keynote of the poem, — not the bird itself, but reflections arising from the sight of it.　The hours spent with Nature, the lessons learned from these, the inspirations received from them, — this makes the theme that the poet develops.

TO THE DANDELION

A poem that in subject may recall Burns's *Daisy*.　Like many of Lowell's other descriptive poems, it goes back to childhood, when our eyes are most open to the beauties about us.

l. 6. **Eldorado.**　Land of gold, the land that the Spanish explorers hoped to find in America.

l. 26. **Sybaris.**　A city noted for luxury and indolence.

Between lines 50 and 51, there were inserted later three additional stanzas.　The dandelion, the poet says, is the type of those "meek charities which make up half the nobleness of life," — "love's smallest coin."　The flower's winged seeds "are like the words of poet and of sage."　Unheeded now, in another age they "take root, and to the gladdened future bear that witness which the present would not heed."　And, like its "common brethren of the ground," the dandelion is full of deep love, with lessons of wisdom that can "soothe life's bitterest ache, and ope Heaven's portals."

A stanza was also added at the end of the poem. The poet says that he can never become really old so long as the dandelion comes with each year to keep him pure with legends of his childhood.

Observe the similarity between this thought and that of lines 13–20 of *The Vision of Sir Launfal.*

AN INCIDENT IN A RAILROAD CAR

The story is clear from the verse. What is the "incident"?

Lines 57 to 67 and 85–88 were omitted in later editions. Can you see any reason for the omission?

l. 84. **Untutored.** Why was this changed later to "unlearned"? What difference in meaning?

Observe the indications in this poem of Lowell's pervading human sympathy, his sense of the nobility of human life, manifest in the *Sir Launfal.*

LINES. SUGGESTED BY THE GRAVES OF TWO ENGLISH SOLDIERS

Lowell, in spite of his strong Americanism, was just, and speaks not unpityingly of those that fell fighting against our country. He passes, however, to take up the other side, with which he ends. The poem lacks unity. That is, it fails to make a clear, single impression. It says many things that are fine, but one result does not stand clear from them. Is this the case with other of Lowell's poems?

THE SHEPHERD OF KING ADMETUS

Admetus was king of Thessaly, a country in Greece. Apollo, the god of music and poetry, had displeased Zeus, the "father of the gods," and was condemned to serve as a mortal in Admetus's house. Lowell has not told the story. He has treated the idea fancifully, hinting, under it all, at the position of the poet and dreamer in the world of to-day. Each great poet, he implies, is like the shepherd, called "good-for-naught" by those about him, but venerated, even worshipped, by the ages following. Has he himself at all in mind, or his own ideals?

THE BEGGAR

Who is the beggar? Of whom does he beg? For what does he ask?

In this poem the main idea is charming, but the execution shows very plainly that it belongs to Lowell's earlier work (1839). "Tempest-shock" and "withering blight," "an angel bright," "fickle fate," etc., come perilously near what is called "fine writing." Yet the thought of the whole is so charming that one can overlook defects of detail.

BEAVER BROOK

This brook was not far from Lowell's home, and one finds him writing of it often in his letters.

l. 3. **The cedar's shadow.** The comparison is to a sun-dial.

l. 6. **The aspen's.** What is there peculiar about the leaves of the aspen ? What other trees are something like it in this ?

l. 12. What is a **chewink** ?

l. 19. **Heaps its small pitcher.** The little mill-pond, where the water is kept ready for the miller's will.

l. 21. **Undine.** See *Indian Summer Reverie*, line 227, also note on p. 112.

The moral does not seem to follow quite naturally from the poem. Do you not notice in Lowell, now and then, a little tendency to "lug in" a moral ? The subject that really moved him here was the beauty of the brook. The other seems an afterthought.

MY LOVE

Written in 1840. It must, consequently, have been inspired by the thought of Maria White, to whom the poet was soon to be married. See what is said of her on p. xxvi. Yet the charm of the poem is that it describes, not one particular woman, but the ideal that many hold in their hearts. Of the thousands that read it, each will think of a different face, yet it is true to all.

THE BIRCH TREE

The light syllable at the end of each line (the so-called *feminine ending*) gives an effect in harmony with the delicate, graceful tree to which the poem is addressed. As you read the poem, try to imagine the tree.

Observe that the fifth line repeats the rhyme-word of the second. The fourth and fifth seem to be meant to rhyme, but the rhymes in several stanzas are far from good. Which stanzas are these?

THE SIRENS

Written at Nantasket on a July day. One wonders if it were on the sand-beaches, or were not rather on the rocks to the south of the beach itself, the creviced cliffs where the poet could have watched the rocky rifts and the seaweed waving its arms. Compare this poem with Tennyson's *Lotos Eaters* and his *Sea-Fairies*. Do you observe any resemblance in tone? What difference in the moral? This poem was written ten years after Tennyson's. What may this show in regard to Lowell's early work?

Sirens were evil creatures that attracted sailors by their sweet singing and by their beauty, — they had the faces of beautiful women, — only to destroy them with vulture-like talons. See the story of Ulysses and note how he avoided their enticements. The sirens in this poem tempt rather into moral peril than into physical. There is an underlying allegory. What do the sirens represent? the sea? Who is the "marinere"?

THE COURTIN'

This is the version as published in the First Series of the *Biglow Papers*. Minor additions and alterations were made later. It is supposed, of course, to be by the rustic poet Hosea Biglow, who is weak in spelling, but strong in human nature. Be sure to imagine the right setting, — the old-fashioned room, on the winter night, with the bashful Zekle trying to get his courage up.

l. 5. **Crooknecks,** crookneck squashes.

l. 7. **Queen's arm,** old-fashioned musket.

l. 8. **Concord.** What happened there in 1775 ?

l. 28. **Ez ef a wager spurred her.** Changed later to " Parin' away like murder." Why is this second form more in character ?

l. 47. **They wuz cried.** That is, the " banns," a formal announcement of the intended marriage, were proclaimed in the meeting-house at " Sunday meeting."

THE CHANGELING

Another poem in which Lowell has in mind the death of his little daughter. A changeling was, in old beliefs, a fairy child, substituted in the cradle for the human child that the fairies stole away. Not that the fairy child was an acceptable substitute. It was generally a shrivelled, weazened, crafty creature that the parents were only too glad to get rid of. Probably the belief resulted from the sudden changes that sickness made in small children. It caused, however, no little cruelty to supposed " changelings," who were often beaten, or even burnt to death, in the hope that the fairies would claim their own and return the stolen child. See Whittier's poem, *The Changeling.*

In this poem Lowell treats the idea fancifully. It is not the fairies, but the angels, that have stolen his child, and they have

left in her place an angel changeling, a "dream-child," a
golden vision of what might have been.

l. 29. **Heavenly Zingari.**   *Zingari* (or, more properly, *Zincali*, as it stood in the first edition) was the Gypsies' name for
themselves.   The application here is fanciful, almost fantastic.
These angels are wanderers, and, like the Gypsies, they carry
away little children.

l. 39. **A violet.** Is this a good figure ?   Do you not feel a
little disappointment in comparing this line with what precedes ?   Is the picture clear ?

l. 52. **Bliss it.** Not a common use, but the meaning is easily
seen, and the effect is pretty.

INDEX

Admetus, 117.

Allston, Washington, 112.

Alms, 97, 98.

Alpha Delta Phi, xix.

Anacreon, 114.

Ἀνήριθμον γέλασμα, 114.

Antislavery movement, xxvi.

Arabesques, 101.

"Ashes and dust," 107.

Aspen, 118.

Atilt, 88.

Auroral, 84.

"Band," The, xxvi.

Barbèd, 106.

"Beautiful Gate," 108.

Biglow Papers, xvi, xvii, xxx–xxxii, 119.

Blanche, Lowell's daughter, 113.

Blazoned, 105.

"Bliss it," 121.

Bower, 109.

Brook, The little, 100.

Burden, 104.

Cambridge in 1830, xi.

"Cap and Bells," 86.

Chalice, 88.

Channing, Prof., xviii.

Chanticleer, 90.

Charles River, xvi, 89.

"Cheeks of Christmas," 102.

Chimney, 102.

"*Collegisse juvat*," 112.

Commemoration Ode, xxxii, xxxiv.

Concord, 120.

Concord, Rustication at, xxiv.

Corbel, 102.

Cowslip, 88.

"Create the world anew," 94.

"Cried" ("they wuz"), 120.

Crooknecks, 120.

Crypt, 101.

"Crystal spars," 100.

Crystalled, 101.

Dana St., 111.

"Devil's booth," 86.

Down, 112.

Drift, 104.

Druid-like, 111.

"Druid wood," 85.
Dryad, 114.

"Earth gets its price," 86.
Eldorado, 115.
Elmwood, xix–xx, 112.

Fable for Critics, xxviii–xxx.
"Fine wheaten bread," 107.
Fretwork, 101.

"Gate, The Beautiful," 108.
Greal (Holy Grail), 92.
Groin, 100.

Hale, Dr. E. E., his recollections
    of Lowell, xxii, xxiii, xxxix.
Hangbird, 109.
Harvardiana, xxiii.
"Heavenly Zingari," 121.
"Hebe Autumn," 110.
"Himself the gate," 108.
Homestead, 112.
Horace, allusion, 112.

"Ice-fern leaf," 101.
Indian Summer, 110.

June, 87.

King Arthur, 92.

"Lashes of light," 101.
Leper, 96, 106.

Leprosie, 107.
Lightsome, 102.
Locust-leaf, 96.
Lowell, James Russell, biograph-
    ies, xxxix; ancestry, xiii; boy-
    hood, xv–xxi; school days, xx-
    xxi; Harvard life, xxi–xxv;
    practice of law, xxiv–xxv;
    marriage, xxviii; daughter's
    death, 113; editor *North Amer-
    ican Review*, xxxiii; lecturer,
    xxxiii; professor of modern
    languages at Harvard, xxxiii;
    minister to Spain and England,
    xxxiii; later life, xxxii–iv;
    Americanism, ix, x; "eternal
    child," xi, xii; humorist, x,
    xi; mystic, xiii, xiv; versifier,
    xiv, xv.
Lowell, Maria White, xxvi, xxvii.

Magellan's Straits, 110.
"Maiden knight," 95.
Mail, 105, 109.
Maize, 89.
May, 87, 89.
Metre, 81, 82, 83, 88, 90.
Mexican war, xxx.
Miscellany, The, xxv.
Mite, 97.
Moral lesson, 113, 114.
"Muses' factories," 111.

Nantasket, Mass., 119.
New Road, The, xv–xvi.
North American Review, The, xxv, xxxii.
" North Countree," 95.
Norton, C. E., xxxix.

Ode on Intimations of Immortality, 84, 85, 86.

Pioneer, The, xxv.
Pitcher-plant, 96.
Potter, Paul, 112.
Preludes, 84, 98, 104.

" Queen's arm," 120.

Robin, American, 89.
Romantic movement in literature, xiv.
Rushes, 94.
Ruth, 110.

Scale, 95.
Seneschal, 104.
" Sharp relief," 101.
" Shed off," 105.
Shrives, 86.
Sign, 105.
Sinais, 85.
Sir Launfal, original, 91–93.
Sirens, 119.

" Snake-like caravan," 106.
Spars, 100.
Startles, 88.
Steel-stemmed, 101.
Stonehenge, 111.
Surcoat, 105.
Swound, 109.
Sybaris, 115.
Symond's Hill, xv, 111.

Tennyson, influence, xxii.
Tents, 95.
Text of poems, xxxviii.
Theme, 84.
" This crust," 108.
" Thread of the all-sustaining Beauty," 98.
" 'Tis only God," 86.
Tree, The, 107.

Under the Willows, xvi, xxxiv, 112.
Undine, 118.
Undine-like, 112.
Unleafed, 100.
Unscarred, 96.

Village blacksmith, 112.
" *Virgilium vidi tantum,*" 112.
Vision of Sir Launfal, xxviii, xxxii, xxxiv–xxxviii; date of publication, xxxix; moral les-

son, xxxvii; object of poem, xxxvi; sources of plot, 93–94; structure of poem, xxxvi; study, spirit, xxxviii; text, xxxix.

Watertown, Mass., 100.
"Weaver Winter," 105.
Whittier, *Snowbound*, 100, 111.

Willows (six old), 112, xvi.
Window-slits, 104.
Winter-palace, 101.
Wold, 99.
Wordsworth, *Ode on Intimations of Immortality*, 84, 85, 86.

Year's Life, A, xxvii.
Yule-log, 103.

Macmillan's

Pocket Series of English Classics

Uniform in Size and Binding

Cloth   25 cents each

Addison's Sir Roger de Coverley. Edited by ZELMA GRAY, East Side High School, Saginaw, Mich.

Andersen's Fairy Tales. Translated from the Danish by CAROLINE PEACHEY and Dr. H. W. DULCKEN. With biographical notes and introduction by SARAH C. BROOKS, Training School, Baltimore, Md.

Arabian Nights. Edited by CLIFTON JOHNSON.

Arnold's Sohrab and Rustum and other Poems. Edited by JUSTUS COLLINS CASTLEMAN, Bloomington High School, Bloomington, Ind.

Bacon's Essays. Edited by Professor GEORGE HERBERT CLARKE, Mercer University, Macon, Ga.

Blackmore's Lorna Doone. Edited by ALBERT L. BARBOUR, Superintendent of Schools, Natick, Mass.

Browning's Shorter Poems. Edited by FRANKLIN T. BAKER, Teachers College, New York City.

Mrs. Browning's Poems (Selections from). Edited by HELOISE E. HERSHEY.

Bryant's Thanatopsis, Sella, and other Poems. Edited by J. H. CASTLEMAN, Michigan Military Academy, Orchard Lake, Mich.

Bunyan's The Pilgrim's Progress, Part I. Edited by Professor HUGH MOFFATT, Central High School, Philadelphia, Pa.

Burke's Speech on Conciliation. Edited by S. C. NEWSOM, Manual Training High School, Indianapolis, Ind.

Byron's Childe Harold. Edited by A. J. GEORGE, High School, Newton, Mass.

Byron's Shorter Poems. Edited by RALPH HARTT BOWLES, Instructor in English in The Phillips Exeter Academy, Exeter, N.H.

Carlyle's Essay on Burns, with Selections. Edited by WILLARD C. GORE, Armour Institute, Chicago, Ill.

Carlyle's Heroes and Hero Worship. Edited by Mrs. ANNIE RUSSELL MARBLE.

Carroll's Alice in Wonderland. Edited by CHARLES A. McMURRY.

Chaucer's Prologue to the Book of the Tales of Canterbury, the Knight's Tale, and the Nun's Priest's Tale. Edited by ANDREW INGRAHAM, Late Headmaster of the Swain Free School, New Bedford, Mass.

Church's The Story of the Iliad.

Church's The Story of the Odyssey.

Coleridge's The Ancient Mariner. Edited by T. F. HUNTINGTON, Leland Stanford Junior University.

Cooper's Last of the Mohicans. Edited by W. K. WICKES, Principal of the High School, Syracuse, N.Y.

Cooper's The Deerslayer.

Pocket Series of English Classics — CONTINUED

Defoe's Robinson Crusoe. Edited by CLIFTON JOHNSON.

De Quincey's Confessions of an English Opium-Eater. Edited by ARTHUR BEATTY, University of Wisconsin.

De Quincey's Joan of Arc and The English Mail-Coach. Edited by CAROL M. NEWMAN, Virginia Polytechnic Institute, Blacksburg, Va.

Dickens's A Christmas Carol and The Cricket on the Hearth. Edited by JAMES M. SAWIN, with the collaboration of IDA M. THOMAS.

Dickens's A Tale of Two Cities. Edited by H. G. BUEHLER, Hotchkiss School, Lakeville, Conn.

Dryden's Palamon and Arcite. Edited by PERCIVAL CHUBB, Vice-Principal Ethical Culture Schools, New York City.

Early American Orations, 1760–1824. Edited by LOUIE R. HELLER, Instructor in English in the De Witt Clinton High School, New York City.

Edwards's (Jonathan) Sermons (Selections). Edited by H. N. GARDINER, Professor of Philosophy, Smith College.

Emerson's Essays (Selected). Edited by EUGENE D. HOLMES, High School, Albany, N.Y.

Emerson's Representative Men. Edited by PHILO MELVYN BUCK, Jr., William McKinley High School, St. Louis, Mo.

Epoch-making Papers in United States History. Edited by M. S. BROWN, New York University.

Franklin's Autobiography.

Mrs. Gaskell's Cranford. Edited by Professor MARTIN W. SAMPSON, Indiana University.

George Eliot's Silas Marner. Edited by E. L. GULICK, Lawrenceville School, Lawrenceville, N.J.

Goldsmith's The Deserted Village and The Traveller. Edited by ROBERT N. WHITEFORD, High School, Peoria, Ill.

Goldsmith's Vicar of Wakefield. Edited by H. W. BOYNTON, Phillips Academy, Andover, Mass.

Grimm's Fairy Tales. Edited by JAMES H. FASSETT, Superintendent of Schools, Nashua, N.H.

Hawthorne's Grandfather's Chair. Edited by H. H. KINGSLEY, Superintendent of Schools, Evanston, Ill.

Hawthorne's The House of the Seven Gables. Edited by CLYDE FURST, Secretary of Teachers College, Columbia University.

Hawthorne's The Wonder-Book. Edited by L. E. WOLFE, Superintendent of Schools, San Antonio, Texas.

Hawthorne's Twice-Told Tales. Edited by R. C. GASTON, Richmond Hill High School, Borough of Queens, New York City.

Homer's Iliad. Translated by LANG, LEAF, and MYERS.

Homer's Odyssey. Translated by BUTCHER and LANG.

Irving's Alhambra. Edited by ALFRED M. HITCHCOCK, Public High School, Hartford, Conn.

Irving's Life of Goldsmith. Edited by GILBERT SYKES BLAKELY, Teacher of English in the Morris High School, New York City.

Irving's Sketch Book.

Keary's Heroes of Asgard. Edited by CHARLES H. MORSE, Superintendent of Schools, Medford, Mass.

Pocket Series of English Classics — CONTINUED

Kingsley's The Heroes: Greek Fairy Tales. Edited by CHARLES A. McMURRY, Ph.D.

Lamb's Essays of Elia. Edited by HELEN J. ROBINS, Miss Baldwin's School, Bryn Mawr, Pa.

Longfellow's Courtship of Miles Standish. Edited by HOMER P. LEWIS.

Longfellow's Courtship of Miles Standish. Edited by W. D. HOWE, Butler College, Indianapolis, Ind.

Longfellow's Evangeline. Edited by LEWIS B. SEMPLE, Commercial High School, Brooklyn, N.Y.

Longfellow's Tales of a Wayside Inn. Edited by J. H. CASTLEMAN, William McKinley High School, St. Louis, Mo.

Longfellow's The Song of Hiawatha. Edited by ELIZABETH J. FLEMING, Teachers' Training School, Baltimore, Md.

Lowell's Vision of Sir Launfal. Edited by HERBERT E. BATES, Manual Training High School, Brooklyn, N.Y.

Macaulay's Essay on Addison. Edited by C. W. FRENCH, Principal of Hyde Park High School, Chicago, Ill.

Macaulay's Essay on Clive. Edited by J. W. PEARCE, Assistant Professor of English in Tulane University.

Macaulay's Essay on Johnson. Edited by WILLIAM SCHUYLER, Assistant Principal of the St. Louis High School.

Macaulay's Essay on Milton. Edited by C. W. FRENCH.

Macaulay's Essay on Warren Hastings. Edited by Mrs. M. J. FRICK, Los Angeles, Cal.

Macaulay's Lays of Ancient Rome, and other Poems. Edited by FRANKLIN T. BAKER, Teachers College, Columbia University.

Memorable Passages from the Bible (Authorized Version). Selected and edited by FRED NEWTON SCOTT, Professor of Rhetoric in the University of Michigan.

Milton's Comus, Lycidas, and other Poems. Edited by ANDREW J. GEORGE.

Milton's Paradise Lost, Books I and II. Edited by W. I. CRANE, Steele High School, Dayton, O.

Old English Ballads. Edited by WILLIAM D. ARMES, of the University of California.

Out of the Northland. Edited by EMILIE KIP BAKER.

Palgrave's Golden Treasury of Songs and Lyrics.

Plutarch's Lives of Cæsar, Brutus, and Antony. Edited by MARTHA BRIER, Teacher of English in the Polytechnic High School, Oakland, Cal.

Poe's Poems. Edited by CHARLES W. KENT, Linden Kent Memorial School, University of Virginia.

Poe's Prose Tales (Selections from).

Pope's Homer's Iliad. Edited by ALBERT SMYTH, Head Professor of English Language and Literature, Central High School, Philadelphia, Pa.

Pope's The Rape of the Lock. Edited by ELIZABETH M. KING, Louisiana Industrial Institute, Ruston, La.

Ruskin's Sesame and Lilies and The King of the Golden River. Edited by HERBERT E. BATES.

Scott's Ivanhoe. Edited by ALFRED M. HITCHCOCK.

Pocket Series of English Classics — CONTINUED

Scott's Lady of the Lake. Edited by ELIZABETH A. PACKARD, Oakland, Cal.

Scott's Lay of the Last Minstrel. Edited by RALPH H. BOWLES.

Scott's Marmion. Edited by GEORGE B. AITON, State Inspector of High Schools for Minnesota.

Scott's Quentin Durward. Edited by ARTHUR LLEWELLYN ENO, Instructor in the University of Illinois.

Scott's The Talisman. Edited by FREDERICK TREUDLEY, State Normal College, Ohio University.

Shakespeare's As You Like It. Edited by CHARLES ROBERT GASTON.

Shakespeare's Hamlet. Edited by L. A. SHERMAN, Professor of English Literature in the University of Nebraska.

Shakespeare's Henry V. Edited by RALPH HARTT BOWLES, Phillips Exeter Academy, Exeter, N.H.

Shakespeare's Julius Cæsar. Edited by GEORGE W. HUFFORD and LOIS G. HUFFORD, High School, Indianapolis, Ind.

Shakespeare's Merchant of Venice. Edited by CHARLOTTE W. UNDERWOOD, Lewis Institute, Chicago, Ill.

Shakespeare's Macbeth. Edited by C. W. FRENCH.

Shakespeare's Twelfth Night. Edited by EDWARD P. MORTON, Assistant Professor of English in the University of Indiana.

Shelley and Keats (Selections from). Edited by S. C. NEWSOM.

Southern Poets (Selections from). Edited by W. L. WEBER, Professor of English Literature in Emory College, Oxford, Ga.

Spenser's Faerie Queene, Book I. Edited by GEORGE ARMSTRONG WAUCHOPE, Professor of English in the South Carolina College.

Stevenson's Treasure Island. Edited by H. A. VANCE, Professor of English in the University of Nashville.

Swift's Gulliver's Travels. Edited by CLIFTON JOHNSON.

Tennyson's Idylls of the King. Edited by W. T. VLYMEN, Principal of Eastern District High School, Brooklyn, N.Y.

Tennyson's Shorter Poems. Edited by CHARLES READ NUTTER, Instructor in English at Harvard University; sometime Master in English at Groton School.

Tennyson's The Princess. Edited by WILSON FARRAND, Newark Academy, Newark, N.J.

Thackeray's Henry Esmond. Edited by JOHN BELL HENNEMAN, University of the South, Sewanee, Tenn.

Washington's Farewell Address, and Webster's First Bunker Hill Oration. Edited by WILLIAM T. PECK, Classical High School, Providence, R.I.

John Woolman's Journal.

Wordsworth's Shorter Poems. Edited by EDWARD FULTON, Assistant Professor of Rhetoric in the University of Illinois.

THE MACMILLAN COMPANY

64-66 FIFTH AVENUE, NEW YORK

Classification
purpose
setting

explain false

16 meaning of dross

17. is lavish a good epithet

18. what picture does ... in lines 3. 4

19. what do grand flower express

an expression.

1 Classification
2 Plot
3 Setting
4 Climax
5 Movement
6 Purpose
7 Theme